THE IMPACT OF A PHD ON DESIGN PRACTICE

THE IMPACT OF A PHD ON DESIGN PRACTICE

International Perspectives

LAURENE VAUGHAN

BLOOMSBURY VISUAL ARTS

LONDON • NEW YORK • OXFORD • NEW DELHI • SYDNEY

BLOOMSBURY VISUAL ARTS
Bloomsbury Publishing Plc
50 Bedford Square, London, WC1B 3DP, UK
1385 Broadway, New York, NY 10018, USA
29 Earlsfort Terrace, Dublin 2, Ireland

BLOOMSBURY, BLOOMSBURY VISUAL ARTS and the Diana logo are trademarks of
Bloomsbury Publishing Plc

First published in Great Britain 2024

A catalogue record for this book is available from the British Library.

A catalog record for this book is available from the Library of Congress.

ISBN: HB: 978-1-3501-5104-8
PB: 978-1-3501-6000-2
ePDF: 978-1-3501-5106-2
ePub: 978-1-3501-5105-5

Typeset by Deanta Global Publishing Services, Chennai, India
Printed and bound in India

To find out more about our authors and books visit www.bloomsbury.com
and sign up for our newsletters.

CONTENTS

FIGURES

THE DESIGNERS

Dr Emma Jefferies holds a keen interest in investigating empathy, well-being, inclusion and the human experience within organizations. She is also a skilled consultant and has collaborated with various clients in diverse industries, emphasizing the importance of prioritizing humans during times of change.

With vast expertise in human-centred design, user experience design and service design, Dr Emma Jefferies is an esteemed design researcher, author and educator. She completed her PhD at Northumbria University, delving into visual literacy within design education.

Dr Daria Loi is a participatory design leader with a passion for enriching people's lives and humanizing technology. Throughout her career she envisioned, built and launched hardware and software solutions in diverse sectors (AI, web, consumer electronics, mobile/client, digital content, VR/XR, cybersecurity, fintech). Her current and past roles include: Principal Engineer at Intel Corporation (2006–19), Head of Experiences and Design at Mozilla (2019–21), Head of Innovation at Avast (2021–22) and Vice President and Head of Design and UX at Fishtail (2022–).

Additional current appointments include: DemocracyLab Board of Directors, Honorary Professor of Practice at Newcastle University Australia, Course5i Client Advisory Board, Columnist for ACM Interactions, DCODE supervisor and Executive Council for CETI Institute. She has conducted research and presented her work in most continents, published 100+ articles and papers, holds fifteen patents and in 2018 was recognized as one of Italy's most inspiring women in tech (InspiringFifty). More at: www.darialoi.com

Dr Chris Marmo is a strategic designer and researcher with nearly twenty years' experience in the design industry in Australia and throughout Asia. He is a co-founder and the CEO at Paper Giant.

He is passionate about the overlaps between people, technology and society, and enjoys mentoring teams through complex problems. Through his career, he has worked across private and public sectors and has delivered research and design outcomes used by hundreds of thousands of people. Chris has degrees in psychology, computer science and a PhD in human–computer interaction.

Dr Dimeji Onafuwa is a design researcher, artist and educator whose interests intersect with transition design, the pluriverse and how design can enable living together. Dimeji earned a PhD in Design from Carnegie Mellon University. His doctoral study investigated commons-based approaches to user experience. He is currently a principal UX research manager at Microsoft. Dimeji co-founded Common Cause Collective, a group of designers exploring transition design methodologies for social impact. He has published papers, written book chapters and delivered several talks on design's role in social justice. As an artist, Dimeji's work features in exhibitions at galleries and museums.

Dr Andrea Siodmok is Dean of Design at RMIT in Melbourne, a member of the 1851 Royal Commission Committee and an external examiner at the Royal College of Art in London. A trained industrial designer with First Class Honours, Andrea has a masters in public policy from the London School of Economics and a PhD in Virtual Reality from Northumbria University. Over more than twenty-five years she has expanded the boundaries of design, developing new design practice in service design, social design and policy design. Andrea has given over one hundred global keynotes on design and technology across five continents. In the UK, Andrea has given evidence at the House of Lords, presented at No. 10 Downing Street and delivered after-dinner speeches at the Law Society and the Palace of Westminster.

In 2010, she was nominated for the top fifty 'Women to Watch' by the Cultural Leadership Programme. In 2015, she received the Royal Society of Arts Bicentenary Medal, and in 2016, an Honorary Doctorate in Civil Law from the University of Northumbria. In 2020, Andrea was listed by Apolitical as 'one of the world's most influential public sector innovators'. For her work in public service, she received an OBE in the Queen's 2021 Birthday Honours.

Dr Reuben Stanton is one of Australia's leading strategic designers and researchers, with twenty years of experience in the design industry in Australia and Japan. His areas of authority include human-centred design practice and its real-world application in both the commercial and public sectors. He believes that design should connect organizations with the communities they serve.

Reuben is particularly dedicated to improving individual and community access to justice by improving people's ability to understand and navigate legal processes and improving representation, regardless of economic or social status.

He holds a PhD in Interaction Design and a Bachelor in Design.

Design researcher academic

Dr Laurene Vaughan is Professor of Design at RMIT University. She served as Founding Dean of the School of Design 2018–22. She was the Nierenberg Chair, Distinguished Professor of

Design, at Carnegie Mellon University, 2012–13. Internationally recognized as a leader in interdisciplinary and applied design research, her research, leadership and creative practice take numerous forms.

Laurene's research investigates the interactive and situated nature of cultural production, place, care and design methods and practices that enable this – both analogue and digital. Her most recent edited collections are *Practice-Based Design Research* and 'Design as a Practice of Care' (2017, 2019).

Portrait of Laurene Vaughan

ACKNOWLEDGEMENTS

The idea for this book commenced around 2019 with the work for the book commencing late that year. I always knew that I was working to a tight timeline, but due to the format of the book, being focused on the interviews, I thought it would all be fine. Then came the beginning of the global transformation in 2020 going through to 2022, because of Covid-19. This had such a profound impact on every aspect of life and work. I've heard this period referred to as the *quiet time*. I quite like this as a way of framing the way that we slowed down, cities became quiet and our pace of connection to others changed to become differently analogue and infinitely more digital.

As a dean of a design school, with a commitment to thousands of students and hundreds of staff, my life didn't feel so quiet on a day-to-day basis. It was dominated by time spent in online meetings, strategizing with my team about what we would do next and how best we could support the students to continue with their studies and each other. I had PhD students located around the world who were trying to complete their studies while also adjusting to their new day jobs. I'm in awe that they made the shifts that they had to, and they completed their studies to be awarded their PhDs during this time.

An advantage of this was that the undertaking of the online interviews with the various participants became easier. We were all far more familiar with the use of Zoom and online platforms for having conversations and for recording them. These occurred in 2021, and I am grateful to all the designers who contributed for their participation in this. Unfortunately, the ongoing insanity that was Covid-19 meant that the pace on the book was slower than I had hoped, and as such, there is a lag between some of the details in the discussions and where the designers are working now. They were all very kind and understanding of my delay in publishing their stories.

This book would not exist without the generous contributions of Andrea Siodmok, Chris Marmo, Daria Loi, Dimeji Onafuwa, Emma Jefferies and Reuben Stanton. I learnt so much from my conversations with them. They are an extraordinary cohort of design leaders globally. The team at Bloomsbury Academic have been equally patient and supportive during this time. Publication due dates have come and gone, but their support has been ongoing. Rebecca Barden, Hattie Morrison and Olivia Davies, thank you.

I would equally like to thank my colleagues who have been supportive and sounding boards about the book from the early days until the end. A special thank you to Andrew Morrison and Cameron Tonkinwise; we had a plan to publish a number of books on design PhDs and have debated this out for some years.

To all my other fellow supervisors and colleagues at RMIT and other institutions around the world, the observations here are the outcome of our years of conversations. I particularly want to note the rich conversations that the RMIT PRS (Practice Research Symposium) programme of biannual reviews has provided me in growing my own approach to working with doctoral students. If you would like to know more about this amazing community of design researchers, please see the documentation of our biannual symposia at practice-research.com.

As a global project, this research has been undertaken on a range of lands of first-nation people in Australia, the United States of America and the United Kingdom. In Australia this has been on the lands of the Wurandjuri people of the Eastern Kuliln Nations, and the lands of the Djaa Djan Wurung and I am grateful for the privilege I have of working and living on these lands. I also wish to acknowledge and thank the RMIT School of Design for the support I have had in completing this book and the sabbatical that allowed me to do this.

Finally, thank you to Hilary Ericksen for her speedy support in copy editing the manuscript and to Ambriehl Khalil for their assistance in compiling the submission.

With gratitude to you all.

Laurene

Introduction

To begin, I would like to be clear that this is not a book about design research, design PhD programmes or how to successfully complete a PhD. It does not provide the reader with a guide for how to transition from being a PhD student to a practising designer with a PhD. The key focus of this book is to share with the reader the experiences of six designers undertaking a PhD, the impact it has had on them as designers and practitioners and how they continue to apply the learnings in their everyday practices.

Design, in all its fields, continues to transform, just as it always has. It is ever in conversation with other socio-technical, cultural and economic transformations. Whether it be the application of new technologies to traditional ways of doing things or the creation of whole new domains in which the design focus is on subjective or ephemeral experience (service or experience design), design practice, and consequently its education, is changed.

Design has many categorizations and classifications. Some list it as a member of the creative arts, with the focus being on 'creativity'; for others it is a professional practice focused on finding solutions to 'wicked problems' (Rittel and Webber 1973) – a key contributor to the innovation economy. New fields of practice, such as user experience design, service design, design anthropology and design research, have become mainstream and are now evident in both design agencies and in industry sectors not thought to be design-oriented, design-informed or design-led.

As the field of design has evolved, so too have the domains of education and training – and expectations of the qualifications that a designer will have. It seems not so long ago that it was unusual for a designer to even have a degree; now, graduate degrees, design MBAs and doctoral programmes have become part of the standard lexicon of design schools globally. Although the design PhD is still contested in some countries, its presence within educational offerings cannot be denied.

What does this mean for a designer, a design practitioner? Traditionally, the PhD has been framed as a qualification for entering academia, for any designer wanting to become a design researcher or professor. This is true, in that a PhD is increasingly required to attain an academic job. But not everyone wants to work in a university or leave their domain of practice, so life for them post-PhD is about the practice of design in a range of contexts.

I have been fortunate to be part of a global of community of design researchers. I've worked with a rich and diverse group of people undertaking their own doctoral studies. I've sat on review panels, attended presentations and examined students from around the globe. I have a passion for all education. From preschool to PhD, I have taught them all, and like many educators, I'm sure, I delight in working with others as their worlds expand through new knowledge and skills. As students learn, so do their teachers – it is a rich relationship, and at doctoral level particularly so. Supervising a doctoral student through the course of their research is the longest relationship that a teacher will have with a student. A shared passion for the research topic drives the beginning of the relationship, and over time, as the relationship changes – as life happens for you both – the growth of the student, as a person and as someone who knows a lot about a topic, is very rewarding to be part of. This has been a privilege throughout my career.

In 2017, I published *Practice-Based Design Research*, also with Bloomsbury. That book was an attempt to map out some of the approaches and structures that different institutions have developed or on which they have focused their doctoral programmes. The final section of that book featured a series of reflections by graduates of design PhD programmes, each detailing their experience or a key moment in their learning that changed the way that they practised and researched. I was struck by the feedback I received from students and other readers about these final chapters. Students found it valuable to hear the real experience of others of 'doing' a PhD. Typically, accounts of doctoral work focus on either the topic of research or the fraught experiences of working with supervisors and advisers, and the overwhelming experience of doing the degree. There is no doubt that undertaking a PhD is incredibly challenging; intellectually, physically and emotionally, you become embedded in your studies. Yet, despite this, it is for most, including myself, one of the most rewarding things to do. I learnt a lot about a topic, about how to research and about myself, too.

This book is an extension of the 2017 publication. Throughout my experience of working with students and speaking to graduates, I have witnessed first-hand the transformation people have been through and the ways that the experience of doing a PhD has impacted on them in their professional careers. There are some accounts of this available for people to read, but typically the accounts are embedded in the research literature and are not something that you can readily access prior to enrolling in a doctoral programme.

Through the conversations with graduate students, my aim here is to provide insights for future and current PhD students, who may be wondering why they would complete a PhD. What value would it offer? Typically, we might think that the catalyst for doctoral education is to be found in the project or the topic of enquiry, but there is more to the doctoral degree than this. It is not unusual for the literature on design education to have an abundance of references to journeys, roads or even gates to be passed through. This is because of the length and focus of the degree, the individual nature of the study experience and submission and the intellectual challenge that the degree requires.

This book is structured around the lived experiences and learnings of six designers who have undertaken PhDs. Drawn from a global network, they undertook their studies in the United Kingdom, Australia and the United States, and they have gone on to have diverse and often global careers, which may still circuit through universities but being an academic is not the focus. These conversations reference both the challenges and the highlights. They indicate similarities in people's experiences and their insights, in different ways, including the catalysts for deciding to undertake a PhD. It should be noted that there is no magic answer or advice in the conversations; they are deliberately reported here as reflective conversations between me and the interviewees. They provide the reader with an opportunity to engage with diverse graduates, and I hope this helps the reader to make an informed decision about what a PhD may offer them beyond deeper knowledge of the topic that currently is driving them. Of course, this collection of conversations is not exhaustive in its representation of people, disciplines, practices or locations.

The possibilities for inclusion are endless and beyond the scope of a book such as this.

The conversations are at the heart of this book and were undertaken in 2021, in the depth of the Covid-19 crisis. Much has changed since then, including many of the contributors taking up new roles, moving countries and expanding their worlds of practice. Where they are now practising may be, therefore, different to what they reference in this text. These five central chapters have been published as conversations, and it is hoped that the 'voice' of each contributor can be heard through the pages, and so too the reality of their experience as a designer – probably like you. You'll find details on each contributor at the beginning of the book in the section named Designers. I have included an introduction to each conversation as a short summary of what is to come.

The chapters before and after the conversations attempt to contextualize the proposition of a design PhD – where it has come from – and then to synthesize some of the common threads that emerge from across the discussions. These are not comprehensive discussions; there are other publications that do this work, which are listed at the end of the book.

In the conversation chapters, a range of terms are used, such as *supervisor, adviser, thesis, project* and *dissertation committee.* These reflect the terminology used in different countries to describe roles, submission formats and modes of examination.

School, faculty and department are also used to position the institutional context of the study inside a university. In this book, they position the experience of each interviewee in relation to place but are not the key focus of the greater conversations about the experience of undertaking the PhD. This can be confusing, and many have attempted to map the diversity of terminology and models, including my colleague Andrew Morrison and me in 2014. Most recently Pieter Jan Stappers and his colleagues (2022) have done this as part of their EU-funded DoCS4Design research project. If you go on to do a PhD, you will soon learn the language and terminology of your specific context.

Within the conversations and in this book, I use the term 'practice', not in relation to the methodology of the designers PhD but with reference to the ongoing and evolving design expertise that each has. As the focus of this publication is on designers who have PhDs who are not academics, I have used the term 'practice' to refer to the evolving design expertise – pre- and post-PhD.

The astute reader will notice, that over the time that it took to write this book, a significant change occurred for me. When I commenced the book I was early in my role as Founding Dean of the School of Design at RMIT. On its completion I have decided to hand the leadership over to someone new while I explore my next contribution to design education and research. Unexpectedly, but very excitingly, Andrea Siodmok has been appointed to the role, leaving industry to take on senior leadership role in academia. This, to me, makes her insights about the importance of design to enable change even more significant. Design leadership and inspiration can happen in many contexts.

1

What is a design PhD?

There are many reasons to undertake a PhD. If you are thinking of embarking on one, you might find that people question why you would do this, especially if you don't want to work in a university or other kind of educational context. If you are an experienced practitioner with an established career as a designer, the questions from friends and colleagues may be even more pressing.

The conversations in this book provide evidence that far beyond the deeper knowledge you acquire through researching a topic for somewhere between three and eight years (depending on where you study and if you are full time or part time), there are many unexpected outcomes from doing a PhD. Learning how to undertake rigorous, innovative research is a fundamental aspect of all PhD programmes, and there are core skills that graduates are expected to have and to be able to apply long after the PhD is complete. Yet, this is only part of the learning that takes place.

Throughout my career as an educator, I have worked in a range of contexts and locations. From primary school education to doctoral supervision, I have always been aligned to peers who understand the experience of learning to be transformational. Whether it is the attainment of skills, deeper knowing and conceptual awareness, the sustaining outcome of learning and formal education is to be challenged and transformed as a person and not always in the manner that we thought that we would be. Our worlds expand, our abilities to do too. What we know, what we can do and who we are all impacted through the learning process.

Doctoral education

The body of literature exploring and endeavouring to define doctoral education across the disciplines is extensive. Many publications seek to understand what a PhD is, different approaches to designing education programmes and what the consequent student experiences are. This is in part a response to the increasing number and type of doctoral programmes offered internationally, and the growth of professional roles that expect a PhD as a qualification for undertaking research. Although this is important work, it is not the focus of this publication. I am seeking to identify, and share with readers, individual experiences of undertaking PhDs and the impact it has had on the careers of those graduates.

In 2022, Sónia Cardoso and colleagues published an extensive literature review of the transformations of doctoral education. The focus of the study was to identify new trends in doctoral education rather than the nuances of the pedagogies and practices of institutions, students and supervisors. They propose that this transformation, as well as the increase and evolution in programmes offered, is a response to our greater move to the 'knowledge society and economy' (Cardoso et al. 2022: 886). This knowledge society is underpinned by the rise of new technologies and, with that, new professions and ways of working. Boundaries between disciplines are increasingly blurred, and research expertise is becoming an expectation in many jobs, even at entry level:

> The traditional model of doctoral education, essentially based on the development of a novel piece of research and the 'apprentice–master' relationship, has gradually begun to give way to other model(s) based on a set of 'ideal' characteristics. (Cardoso et al. 2022)

These new models include a focus on employability of graduates, critical methodologies and new design approaches that include practice- and problem-based enquiries. Education is always responsive to the context of its time, whether it is social, cultural or technological education. The way we teach and learn moves in step with the evolution of the knowledge society and economy.

Educational change at any level occurs only with due debate and interrogation, and educational systems can morph and change in response to many external factors, from government policy to international networks of academic institutions. The evolution of design education, the degrees offered and the industry education is aligned with are important parts of the picture. New technologies and transformed ways of working and connecting (accelerated during Covid-19), along with the rise in design schools offering PhDs, have had a significant impact on the opportunities for designers to undertake PhDs, both in design and in other fields.

Through this, we have seen a greater recognition of design, beyond the material practices of designing and making. Integrating practice that links to deeper forms of 'design knowing' (Cross 2007) underpins many studies. The work of Donald Schön (1983) on reflective practice and the integration of knowing and doing has been a basis for much of the founding studies and learnings in the field. Since then, a significant body of work on design methods and design research has evolved and been published, from participatory design to co-design, design anthropology, user experience design, service design, and so on. Each of these domains of design practice, research and curriculum opens new ways of undertaking research and of embedding research into industry and cultural contexts. Most recently, the decolonizing design movement and an increased awareness of culturally diverse design paradigms are resulting in exciting domains of research and practice.

Maturing the field

As design practices mature as academic disciplines, so too do the educational systems that are aligned with it.

The primary focus of a doctoral degree has been to develop the research expertise and capacity of a graduate, thus preparing them for a career as either a researcher or an academic. In the sciences, this includes working in industry research facilities. In many countries, the PhD is the highest qualification in education framework, and in some countries, such as Australia, it is referred to as a 'research-training degree', that is, a degree that is focused on developing a student's research expertise. It is for this reason that, to date, there has been little curriculum that has focused on developing a student's expertise beyond introducing them to research methodologies and methods and a good grounding in ethics. The rest of their training takes place through a 'master–student' model of learning. In the sciences, this happens in the labs and workspaces of the more senior researchers. In the humanities, it is through dialogue and meetings with the supervisor or adviser throughout the duration of the study.

In the area of arts and design, a hybrid model of training is evolving, depending on the research focus and the institution in which the student is enrolled. In some instances, the models and expectations of research progress and outcomes have been driven by those used in other disciplines. Over the past thirty years it has been a slow process of maturation, resulting in global offerings of research degrees and graduates of programmes. Yet this has resulted in a robust discourse in the university sector, and with certain industry bodies, as to the most appropriate model and approach for design education. Increasingly, the discourses of practice have become dominant, which is in part congruent with the increasing professionalization of design disciplines and industries. As the field becomes more assured of its role in and contribution to society, design methods and literacies are recognized as rigorous and a valid educational approach to research degrees.

There are, of course, core skills and expertise that an advanced researcher in any discipline should be able to demonstrate, even within different knowledge paradigms. A point at which this becomes interestingly evident is in the examination process. Through the many different (and at times contested) models of examination across the global education sector, at its heart is the need to ensure students have the same core capabilities: they are able to design a research study that is rigorous, well structured and responds to work that already exists (methodology and research design); they can review the work of others in the area and position their own research in relation to it (literature review); and they can present their research findings clearly and to the appropriate audience (thesis/project). As someone who has examined many PhDs, these are the common competencies that I am asked to evaluate, even when the mode of examination differs. They are what we might call 'core competencies' of a graduate from an advanced research-training degree. This expertise they will be able to apply to future projects in many different contexts.

Writing is an important component of nearly all PhD submissions, and it is also crucial to research communication in the form of reports and academic publications. Research communication, too, is evolving, partly in response to new technologies and forms of accessible communication formats, such as short-form videos. New disciplines are also expanding research communication to include exhibitions, performances and graphic communication, such as diagrams. The PhD submission has moved far beyond the conventional long-form written thesis, and the students at the vanguard of this transformation should be acknowledged for their commitment and bravery.

Despite still being positioned as a research-training degree, with the focus on building research skills, there is growing awareness of and concern for expanding competencies in graduate students (Cardoso et al. 2022: 895). These relate to the employment and post-study skills that graduates will need in conjunction with their research capability. At one time, the key rationale for a PhD was to become an academic, and the experience of working in the institution, the university, was a form of embedded or situated learning; the student became familiar with the ways of the institution, perhaps teaching part time, and on graduating they would make their way into the academic world. In North American PhD programmes, there continues to be a focus on developing students' teaching skills as part of their studies, and PhD students make up an important quota of the teaching staff. There is also a rich public conversation exploring the nature of the design PhD (naphdbydesign.com), and I recommend engaging with their documentation.

But what happens when the student doesn't want to become an academic? What if they want to work outside the university system? What if they are already working in industry and want to use the PhD as a means to deepen their knowledge about and passion for a topic? This is the case for an increasing number of doctoral students and it needs to be, as the number of PhD students globally far outstrips the opportunities for employment in the university sector.

What training do these students need beyond developing their research and writing skills? Increasingly, institutions are providing students with additional courses and resources to support them in developing other professional competencies and skills. It is a synergistic response to the realization that as practice and workplace expectations evolve, so too must the university courses that prepare students for employment in a broader labour market context. Often these courses engage interpersonal, communication, collaboration and professional behaviour domains (writing a CV, interviewing for a role, for example), offerings that are often referred to as 'soft skills' and become a common theme in the conversations in the following chapters. In many ways, these are skills that graduates of any educational programme are expected to have, and they indicate the PhD is no longer purely about building research ability. It is also about becoming a professional researcher in a wider context. Understanding is expanding regarding what it is to train someone to undertake research and to become a researcher.

The conversations

The following conversational chapters provide insights into the experiences of five individuals during their PhD journeys. None of them commenced their studies with a desire to work in a university at the PhD's completion. As you will see, the focus of the conversations is not on design or research, but rather on how their experience of a research-training degree has informed their ongoing practice. Most of the designers commenced their design study and practice as either industrial or communication/graphic designers. Over time they have all moved into new areas focused on either new technologies or the application of design methods and practices to new areas such as the design of services, strategy or policy.

I have recently been immersed in Lisa Grocott's *Design for Transformative Learning: A Practical Approach to Memory-Making and Perspective Shifting* (2022). She takes the reader through a deep interrogation of the transformational nature of learning. A professor with a key interest in pedagogy and learning, Grocott's reflections, conversations and case studies consider ways that teachers might design transformational learning experiences. These are experiences that reoriente the learner, challenge their belief systems and open them to new ways of learning. Quoting Jack Mezirow, she notes it is a 'disorientating dilemma' (Grocott 2022: 26) that can often sit at the heart of learning design.

Throughout my career I have sought to create learning opportunities for doctoral students that both deepen their knowledge and disorientate them from what they felt assured of. A research degree enables a space for deep thinking, and this can resonate at the most fundamental level. As I reflected on the many insights of Grocott's book and the generous contributions of the designers who participated in the conversations presented in the following chapters, it became clear this book offers something aside from mining the relationships between student, teacher and institution. Its focus is the transformation of the individual through the course of research and the impact of this on them as people. It is not a tale of how to design a better PhD programme; it is a series of accounts about the transformation each participant has experienced through their learning.

A research degree enables a space for deep thinking, and this can resonate at the most fundamental level.

Portrait of Emma Jefferies

2

Building resilience and confidence

Laurene Vaughan speaks with Emma Jefferies

The lifelong outcomes of doctoral education for graduates span the personal and the professional. The duration, depth of focus and individual passion that drives the pursuit of answers and insights is fundamental to this. In this conversation, Dr Emma Jefferies reflects on the ways in which her research laid the foundation for her commitment to empathy as an enabler of better experiences for herself and others.

Emma commenced her doctoral studies immediately after her undergraduate degree. As she notes, this is not so common in design but very common in the sciences. She had a passion to know more about visual literacy and how this could be used to enable better communication for people from diverse backgrounds. In her own case, she is dyslexic, and visual tools were a means for her to understand and communicate. Through her research, she extended this capacity and trialled the use of tools in her fieldwork.

In the course of the conversation, Emma identifies resilience and curiosity as the two key things that PhD process instilled in her. Curiosity is an essential but perhaps underexplored disposition that all good researchers and designers need to have. Curiosity slows you down; you can't be curious and jump to a conclusion. Underpinning Emma's curiosity is a structured practice of reflection, which she uses personally and in her various professional roles. She refined this skill through her research training and exposure to 'action learning', with its observe, plan, act and reflect cycles.

After completing her studies, Emma continued collaborating with individuals she met during her PhD, and she embarked on a global adventure, working in design studios across the world. Concurrently, she worked alongside Professor Joyce Yee and Dr Lauren Tan as co-authors of a book on the transformation of design and the emergence of new design practices, in the 2010s, and expanded her understanding beyond conventional Eurocentric design practices, focusing on empathy as a means of understanding people's needs. The outcome was the book *Design Transitions: Inspiring Stories. Global Viewpoints. How Design Is Changing*, with Joyce Yee and Lauren Tan (Laurence King Publishing, 2013). Emma also established the design consultancies The Design Doctors and then WEmindset®, an educational consultancy focused on the practice of empathy, and now works as a management consultant in the United States.

Emma's reflections and insights illustrate how her PhD, including the people and context she studied in, the opportunities that it afforded and the bravery and commitment she brought to her study, supported her in realizing her design practice career. As she notes, the girl from a small fishing village in northern England has gone on to become a global leader in the future domains of design practice. You can hear more on the *Story of Emma Jefferies* on the Creative Leadership Podcast (2021).

Laurene: Can you tell me when did you complete your PhD?

Emma: In 2010, at Northumbria Design School in Newcastle in the UK.

Laurene: It was in design?

Emma: Yes it was. It's important to recognize and acknowledge the pioneering efforts of those who have come before us. Back when I was doing my design PhD, it was a very new field, and Professor Bob Young had established a group of PhD researchers at Northumbria University's School of Design. I remember attending quantitative and qualitative methods sessions and feeling like they didn't quite align with the ethos of research through design, which involves deep reflection, understanding people, problems and contexts to suggest improvements for future design. Despite the challenges we faced as a PhD cohort, it was also a space for exploration, and I believe that everyone who went through the process helped forge a new path for those who followed.

Laurene: What were you doing when you decided to do the PhD?

Emma: I still vividly remember the moment when Professor Bob Young asked me if I wanted to do a PhD in visual literacy, just as I was about to complete my undergraduate degree at twenty-one. I didn't hesitate and jumped at the opportunity to delve deeper into my fascination with the subject. I was determined to explore visual literacy at an advanced level. Being dyslexic myself, I knew that understanding this topic would not only be personally fulfilling but could also bring new insights and perspectives to the field.

Laurene: What field of design was your undergraduate degree in?

Emma: Multimedia Design MA.

Laurene: Moving straight from that into three years of PhD intensity is challenging. But did you complete the PhD in three years?

Emma: I completed my undergraduate degree in 2003 and obtained my doctorate in 2010, which occupied most of my twenties. Pursuing a PhD was a challenging journey since there was no clear road map to follow. I initially followed what I thought was the right path, but I soon discovered that it may not be the optimal path. As a result, I adapted my approach and explored alternative paths until I found the strategies that worked best for me.

Laurene: Since completing your PhD what have you been doing?

Emma: My passion lies in exploring diverse cultures and understanding people better. During my PhD programme, Professor Joyce Yee asked me about my career goals, and I shared my aspiration of contributing to the global design industry's evolution by studying practices in emerging markets. This revelation provided me with a clear purpose, driving me to succeed in my doctoral studies. This clarity of purpose served as a powerful motivator throughout my doctoral journey. Additionally, we had the privilege of hearing from influential speakers such as Tim Brown from IDEO, Engine, and Livework during DOTTO7 (2007) in Newcastle, an initiative led by John Thackara and supported by the UK Design Council. This event explored how design could facilitate sustainable living, and it left a lasting impact on my approach to design leadership.

After completing my PhD, I began strategizing how to pursue my goal of working globally. During a conversation with Joyce, she suggested that I co-author a book on how design is transforming and document the ongoing transition. Though initially uncertain, I recognized the importance of showcasing design's value and the impact it has on both businesses and communities. To further inspire design research, I created a Google Map named 'The Hitchhiker's Guide to Design Research' and encouraged people to share companies that inspired them. Alongside this, I established my consultancy, The Design Doctors, to provide design teams with a space to use their creative tools on themselves. Reflection time is often scarce as companies are always racing against time to implement their designs. However, it's critical for determining actions and creating value through reimagining design practices and values.

As a leader, my global design research adventure started with an invitation from the DesignThinkers Group in the Netherlands to collaborate with Arne van Oosterom and Marjo Staring. I witnessed the incredible impact of their design practices in business, helping companies understand their true value and prioritize customer-centricity. In Brazil, I worked with Voel and Eduardo Loureiro to transition their design company into a strategic design practice, leveraging the prototyping mindset and human connection values that Voel exemplified. Finally, in India, I learned from design entrepreneur Sonia Manchanda at Idiom, where the Jugaad innovation approach demonstrated how to make meaningful market disruptions with limited resources. These experiences were invaluable and continue to inform my design practices today.

As a means to ground myself after extensive travels, I made the decision to return to Newcastle. There, I worked as a consultant in various innovation companies, assisting them in developing their practices. Afterward, I spent five years as a Senior User Researcher in the UK government. I now live in the US; I have launched my own company, Wemindset®, centred around my passion for empathy and inclusion. Now I am in a full-time role in management consulting. I see the value of working at the intersection of other disciplines, particularly in the areas of E.S.G. and healthcare. I believe that by combining our skills and expertise, we can create meaningful solutions that benefit individuals, organizations and society as a whole.

Laurene: It seems you have been on a rich and varied journey since completing your PhD, and your knowledge of and approach to design has been deepening. Having done the PhD, in what ways do you think the PhD has influenced where you are now? Not in terms of content (although your focus on empathy seems to have evolved through your education experience) but in terms of becoming the practitioner who decides to set up a consultancy or a company that focuses on empathy necessarily. I suppose what I'm curious to know is, what is the correlation for you between the content of your PhD and the focus of your ongoing practice?

Emma: Reflective practice was first introduced to me during my PhD programme, and since then, I've found that following the simple steps of plan, do, reflect has been immensely helpful. Through the process of conducting research and journaling about my work with design students, I became much more self-aware. I realized that by stepping back from my actions and reflecting on them, I could make changes to improve myself. This self-reflection has become a regular practice throughout my career, and it's a skill that I bring to the organizations I work with. Many people are uncomfortable with pausing to reflect, but I believe that building reflection into one's routine can lead to greater agility and positive change. As an empathy practitioner, I've seen the benefits of incorporating small habits of change into teamwork, which encourages people to reflect and gain self-awareness. By valuing reflective practice, I've found that I'm able to create environments that foster personal growth and positive change.

My dyslexia has been a crucial factor in shaping my perspective and way of thinking, even before I pursued my PhD studies. Despite my brain often racing too quickly and bouncing off in different directions, I've learned that there are always different ways of seeing things and moving them around. Through self-reflection, I began to uncover new aspects about myself and my dyslexia. For example, I used to walk very quickly everywhere I went, until I noticed my Brazilian colleagues walking slowly. Walking with them allowed me to slow down my thoughts and gain new insights. Although I've been told that my brain moves ten times faster than others, self-reflection and slowing down have enabled me to discover new interconnections and achieve personal growth.

Laurene: That's fascinating and a great way of thinking through an approach to practice. To me what you're saying about your practice and the focus on empathy, which itself requires time and connectivity, to identify what is not, as much as what is. I'm fascinated by how you have proposed that is counter to the current discourses of agility. Fast, with an imperative for disruption. We live in a time when speed is good. Speed and the being so agile that we're missing the point.

When you were sharing this, it made me think of a stone skipping across water and barely touching. Just always skipping to the next thing without actually understanding the full impact of what's in the moment, of what you're doing and the impact that it's having because you move on before you know what you did.

Emma: Yes.

Laurene: That very strong future focus. You've mentioned it a couple of times now, so I'm interested to know how important do you think a person with dyslexia was for your learning? I'm not wanting to think of it as you had to overcome it. I don't want to look at it from that perspective. But what did it give you? Because it seems that from what you're telling me it's giving you something particular to be able to bring to others.

Emma: I fully embrace my dyslexia, which has given me a unique perspective on work and problem-solving. I approach tasks by sketching out my ideas, allowing me to connect the dots in a way that is natural to me and encourages collaboration among team members. This method not only helps me to create new ideas but also enables others to visualize their contributions to the project.

As I've journeyed through life, I've come to realize that society often imposes limiting narratives and expectations upon us. However, I refuse to be constrained by such boxes and have always sought to create my own path. By being open to the endless possibilities and constantly exploring my passions, I have learned to break free from the societal norms and expectations. Sketching and reflective practice have been instrumental in my journey, and I've even used sketch conversations during my PhD studies to further my understanding.

Laurene: Is that how you discovered the method?

Emma: I have developed my unique approach to tackling challenges that involves mind mapping and visual sketchbooks. During my PhD, I utilized these techniques to think about complex issues on a larger scale, such as finding ways to enhance people's visual literacy. In fact, I even incorporated visual maps into my viva process, which I redesigned to accommodate my dyslexia. This experience taught me the importance of resilience, as I discovered that stress can exacerbate dyslexia and diminish cognitive capacity.

Laurene: Did you name this in your PhD submission? Did you name it in the dissertation and in the viva that it was about visual literacy and methods of visual literacy? Did you share that you were dyslexic and that this was a lens that you were bringing to the work?

Emma: I must admit that I had not previously considered a certain perspective. While discussing my work with my supervisors, this perspective was present in our conversations, but it was not explicitly identified as a lens through which I brought my material together.

Laurene: Have you ever had conversations with other people who are dyslexic about their approaches to communicating? Did you share with them your visual method?

Emma: I am passionate about exchanging knowledge and techniques with others, which is why I posted my methods on my YouTube channel after completing my PhD. I received numerous messages from people who found my approach to writing and synthesis helpful, and I am always eager to assist in any way possible. My three-layered approach to writing, which involves getting everything down, synthesizing critical writing paths and finalizing the draft, has helped to reduce my stress levels, and others have found it useful as well. I have to give credit to my amazing tutor, Pat Evans; she really encouraged me to use the methods and techniques that come naturally to me, and she would help me with the spelling. How did you do your PhD process?

Laurene: It seems to me that you can say you don't conform but it seems like it's a strength. This is a rigorous writing process.

Emma: It really is. Yes. Because you can then see new opportunities and new places to explore.

Laurene: For me when I was writing up my PhD I had to draw it first before I could write it. I had access to the fashion school where they had very large cutting tables, their workbenches. So over the summer holiday I took over one of the studios. I had to lay out on large sheets of paper – every table was a chapter and on the chapter table I had to draw what it was about. I had printouts of the images I would use. I had lines around it would say who the key reference was going to be, what literature it was going to be and then how I was doing it. I worked my way through the three project chapters.

But hanging in the middle of the room was this spiral structure because the whole proposition was around labyrinths and creativity is a kind of labyrinth mind process. I was trying to make a 3D model of a labyrinth and one of my advisers walked into the room and she just went 'I can't stay in here. It is overwhelming', and she just left. I can't work from a blank screen, I needed to see it. So yes, I completely understand your need to make things visual. Do you think that this capacity that you've just been describing about and the methods you've developed for how to work with other people supported you in working across cultural contexts?

Emma: It comes back to curiosity. During my PhD journey, I realized that my thought process differed greatly from that of others. I am passionate about learning new things and exploring the ways in which others think. Every time I worked in a new environment, I embraced the opportunity to gain new knowledge, even when it was challenging. There were instances where the context was vastly different from my comfort zone. I found it necessary to delve deep into understanding the perspective of others while maintaining a sense of curiosity. Empathy is crucial, but it is also essential to have the curiosity to ask, 'Why is it like that?'

When I had the chance to work in Saudi Arabia, I recall my deep curiosity about the women's floor in the office and the real and perceived limitations on women's movements and actions. Despite the preconceived notions I had about Saudi Arabia and women, getting to know the people there helped me strip away the layers of societal norms imposed on them and appreciate them as human beings. I believe that maintaining curiosity can help us appreciate the uniqueness of individuals and foster a culture of learning. By embracing different perspectives and understanding the experiences of others, we can build more inclusive and empathetic teams.

I have always held the belief that understanding different cultures is crucial. Whenever I travelled to a new country, I found it fascinating to immerse myself in their way of life. Luis Arnal's talk at the EPIC conference in 2015 in Brazil resonated with me, particularly his idea that experiencing other people's lives extends our own. Life moves quickly, and by experiencing different cultures, we can gain a more profound understanding of the world through other people's eyes. This, in turn, helps us reflect on our own lives and how we show up in the world.

I find the idea of understanding cultures and how people show up in the world incredibly fascinating. As a leader, it is crucial to have a broad perspective and to appreciate the diverse perspectives of those around us. By cultivating an understanding of different cultures, we can build more inclusive and empathetic teams, and ultimately drive more significant impact in our work.

Laurene: Do you think if you had gone straight to practice that you would have got where you are now?

Emma: I believe that personal growth and development are crucial components of success. My own experience pursuing a PhD programme allowed me to meet individuals from diverse backgrounds and cultures, an opportunity that was particularly impactful as I grew up in a small fishing village in northeast England with a predominantly white culture. Through the PhD programme, I was able to gain a newfound sense of curiosity and open-mindedness, which inspired me to seek out even more diverse experiences. Additionally, the space for self-reflection provided by the programme helped me to develop the resilience and confidence necessary to create my own path in life.

Laurene: That's great. I think you're right. It's not something people expect. You've shared with me that you've both learnt methods or a way of practising and a domain of practice to work in. But also it's who you are which is then intimately connected, I would say to the empathy component too. I think writing a PhD is the hardest thing you can ever do. All sorts of things are hard but in terms of intellectual work and creative work I think that the PhD because it's the one time you spend so long on a single project.

You never spend that amount of time focused on one thing, interrogating it and designing the way that is best to interrogate it, and then you know it's going to be examined for its contribution to knowledge and rigour. It's incredibly difficult and some people don't make it through it. For some people it's too hard. It throws up too many things personally and a lot happens in the seven years, six years, three years. It's a long time with your supervisor and a lot happens in your life. It's not like being an undergraduate student. It's an intensive yet rewarding thing. It's been interesting to hear you talk to how it's built in you that resilience and that adventurousness as well because you seem like an adventurer to me.

Emma: Yes.

Laurene: To travel to distant lands from home, from a small fishing village in the northeast of England. It's a long way to Brazil and the cultural differences that each of those places brought. Do you think that your understanding of and your explorations in visual literacy have supported you in being able to work in these very different cultural contexts?

Emma: I believe that questioning our assumptions and seeing the world through different perspectives is essential for growth. During my PhD, I explored the social aspect of visual literacy, which highlighted that each person has their own unique way of understanding and interpreting the world around them. It's impossible for me to fully understand someone else's point of view, but we can guide each other through asking questions and understanding the shifts in our experiences. To help students develop self-awareness of their own visual development and working tools, I created characters based on their behaviour, such as Mrs Hudson, Dr Watson and Sherlock Holmes. These personas provided a framework for reflection and helped me identify where I might be limiting myself or overanalysing. Even dressing up as the characters to present them at the end of the work was a way of emphasizing the importance of understanding different perspectives. I believe that by recognizing and respecting the unique experiences and perspectives of others, we can foster a more inclusive and collaborative environment.

Laurene: Thank you. I think you've really given me a very different aspect of this project and this research in terms of what you've shared around what you've learnt around your PhD and how it's gone on. Is there anything else you would like to add in?

Emma: I'm curious, what's your sense of where PhDs are going now? Because it was the very early days in 2003 when I started, is there more structure around the PhD now? Are people's expectations changing as to why they're doing it and what they will get out of it?

Laurene: I think with that there is a growing recognition that people with PhDs have the capacity to contribute to organizations and work in a different way to a designer at an undergraduate level. That there's another level of critical thinking, another level of insight and interconnectivity because things you know when you do a PhD is in the beginning you know you know nothing. You've got a hunch. Halfway through/two-thirds of the way through you think I've got it. I know what it is, and I know everything about this topic. I've got it. Then at the end you realize I know this little bit of this really big thing. You kind of learn humility, intellectual humility and as well as you said curiosity.

Portrait of Dimeji Onafuwa

3

Establishing voice

Laurene Vaughan speaks with Dimeji Onafuwa

There are many reasons people undertake a PhD. Whether a career necessity, an employment opportunity through a grant or simply driven by desire to research a specific topic, the pathway to doctoral study can take many forms. In the following conversation, Dr Dimeji Onafuwa shares the catalyst for his own doctoral studies and the unexpected outcomes that emerged from it. Dimeji had a rich and diverse career and educational background prior to entering the doctoral programme in the School of Design at Carnegie Mellon University (CMU). As he notes, he was the first graduate of the inaugural cohort of the university's Transition Design PhD, through a practice programme.

As our conversation unfolds, Dimeji shares insights about the differences between his experience of an MBA in management and subsequent employment experience and his post-PhD employment in the tech sector in North America. Dimeji entered his doctoral studies enthused by the opportunity to develop design strategies and approaches to enable him to contribute to the social innovation sector and issues relating to Nigeria, his home country. But this was all to change. He has devised a post-PhD career with multiple channels of contribution and impact, including teaching, presenting and publishing, while working in industry. Social change and a contribution to equity continue to inform his work, and he explains that the experience of undertaking the PhD was essential to developing communication strategies to both find and be the voice of those that we design for.

Throughout his reflections, Dimeji rarely discusses the content of his doctoral research; rather, he is interested in the expertise he has developed to understand the systemic nature of change and the impact that power, conventions and reticence have on meaningful innovation in business and its outcomes. Hinted at in his comments is a questioning of efficiency over meaning. Threaded through his conversation is his commitment to being a good colleague and contributor and advocating for those who aren't able to speak and for those often overlooked.

Design practice and research increasingly embraces alternative and at times subversive ways of initiating change, from Dan Hill's articulation of Trojan horses (2012) or Gill Wildman's embrace of the trickster (2021) as embodied strategies to give voice to the voiceless in projects. Dimeji names his practice one of advocacy, but rather than being advocacy through design, his is a practice of advocacy *within* design. There is no doubt that his experience of being an African Black man in the United States has been a basis for his commitment to diversifying design projects and business practices. Through his PhD, he has been able to develop the communication tools and to build the respect that supports him in this work.

Advocacy is a specific area of leadership. It demands empathy, awareness, bravery and a strategic approach to participating in the conversations that matter and where change begins.

Although we didn't get to talking about it in this conversation, transition design, with its focus on systems design and thinking, undoubtedly would have provided Dimeji with an appreciation for the long-term focus that advocacy demands. Resilience in the face of obstacles and empowerment through educational achievement are present in Dimeji's reflections on his transformation and ongoing growth as a member of the international design community.

Laurene: To begin, could you share with me what you did prior to undertaking your PhD? What was your background knowledge and expertise that you brought to the PhD?

Dimeji: I have – and as many would claim, a diverse background. I have undergraduate degrees in both art and design. I was initially trained as a painter, and I also undertook an undergraduate design degree. I worked as a designer in an agency for about five years. Then, I decided to start my own design studio in the southeast of the United States. I ran that studio for about ten years and while I was running the studio, I went on and earned an MBA. The catalyst for doing the MBA was that I was beginning to think about where the intersections of design and business were. Particularly what are the ways in which design might essentially influence how businesses think about their work. I had stumbled on Roger Martin's book (*The Design of Business*, 2009) but I did not have the luxury to go to Stanford (D-School) or any of those graduate schools, so I went and got an MBA in management.

Once I completed that, I continued to work in design and then I had a moment where I started to explore what was it that I wanted to do next? I knew how designers solve problems – I'd been working as a designer for a while; I knew how to articulate the way designers solve problems to business, but I felt there was something missing or more. I thought of it as a third there, a way to practice overlapped with where I was from. I was born in Nigeria and there were multiple potential social challenges in that country, and I was beginning to try to understand what role design could play in solving the problems, or at least in framing problems in such a way that we can actually solve them. So that was where I started to explore the PhD.

While I was exploring doing a PhD, I worked in marketing, I worked as an operations director for a small marketing company and it was through that work that I essentially transitioned to Carnegie Mellon and started the PhD.

Laurene: What did you imagine the PhD would afford you in the beginning? So, trying to think back at the beginning, how did you think it would help you find this new way of designing for impact?

Dimeji: I remember being invited to a conference for historically underrepresented folks where they were trying to encourage them to get a PhD in business, it was called the PhD Project. It was sponsored and you were nominated for it. I remember walking in the halls of the conference, and I was asking questions to the different universities and having conversations with them about what I wanted to do. I was very clear about what I wanted to do, and I was trying to understand where design met economics or where it met social impact. I think it was mostly design, economics and social impact with a focus on something that would actually help me do this in practice.

I remember folks telling me that this wasn't possible in North America. It was serendipitous that I found the PhD in Design at Carnegie Mellon University (CMU). I felt that being able to do those things and working at the intersections of those three areas (design, economics and social) would allow me to be able to work in social impact and find ways in which I could explore the socio-technical implications of social innovation. I think that was my thinking. I was thinking about working for an organization like IDEO.org or working for a non-profit or, essentially, continue to carry on the work of social impact through design. Those were my intentions going into the PhD programme, and boy did they change over the course of my study.

Laurene: Did doing the PhD achieve your ambition in terms of who you wanted to be and enable you to become the designer you wanted to be at the end?

Dimeji: I will say yes and no. Maybe a better way to put it is to say 'indirectly'. By that I mean, I am not in social innovation, I am not working in design for social impact and I am not working – as my day job – as a transition designer and it was a Transition Design PhD that I did at CMU. I was the first graduate in the transition design programme, and I am not working as a transition designer as a core job description everyday, but I am carrying on the tradition in many ways.

I am teaching coursework as an adjunct professor at Emily
Carr University of Art and Design, and I have founded a
collective of designers that are employing transition design
methodologies to address big problems in the city of Seattle.
I am bringing these ideas – sometimes in a limited way –
into the conversation and trying to change the way designers
working in tech think about the work that they do.

So indirectly, yes, the PhD has allowed me to accomplish
certain parts of my ambition but when you think about my
core work on a day-to-day, no, it didn't translate. It didn't
map directly to the core work that I do. As a matter of fact, I
looked for work in that space and I couldn't find it. I wasn't
accepted. I would go past the interview stage and not get a
job offer. I was very deliberate about working in that space
but unfortunately, life had other intentions.

Laurene: In doing the PhD you learned a lot about Transition
Design as an approach to design practice, but what do you
think you learned in a more broader practise orientation?
Because if you're not working in social innovation
specifically, what do you bring as a PhD graduate to your
current role, which is in a tech company?

Dimeji: I think a couple of things. I have been messing
around in the space by working on a set of pluriversal
design principles for practitioners. I have been bringing a
lot of transition design to my practice. Transition Design

is a systemic approach to problem-solving. I think being able to think systemically and then still find ways to distil the problems into the level interaction (something with which designers are more familiar) has been a useful skill I acquired during my doctoral study.

I think another thing that Transition Design does is to bring the wicked problems we face – problems that relate to inclusion, social justice and other consequences – into a practice that often ignores these issues. I believe that designers must continue to reflect on Anne-Marie Willis's Ontological Design, her admonishment that that 'design designs', meaning design continues to transform and have impact beyond the initial outcome. Designers must commit to telling such a story to those organizations that are increasingly bearing the responsibility for remaking our world.

Prior to working at my current company, which is Google, I worked at Microsoft on the future of work. That project allowed me to apply a lot of the stuff I studied in the PhD programme. It allowed me to think about the future of work more holistically. Case in point, my dissertation really touched on the commons, and I was thinking about collective livelihoods that are intertwined. I was trying to think about how people work collaboratively to solve a problem together even if it's just around how we work and what does that look like? So, there are lots of things that I can bring, and I feel like I brought, from my PhD pursuits to every day at work.

Laurene: You have two undergraduate degrees, an MBA and then the PhD. Now, for many people who work in the professions, the MBA – sometimes a DBA – is actually enough. Do you think there is something different that you learnt – and that you now bring too, as a member of a team and as a leader – through having a PhD as well as an MBA? Do you think there's any kind of synergy, or not, in that?

Dimeji: I think the PhD more than the MBA. One of the things that the MBA – thinking back on the MBA that I earned – does is that it allows me to understand the limitations of business or thinking in terms of a business strategy primarily. I feel like the MBA allowed me to understand the consequences and the limitations of doing just that. I think the PhD allows me to really, essentially, apply my research and learning to everything. The deeper thinking, systems thinking and critical work that you do in a PhD allows you think about the stakeholders that the work you're doing might potentially impact. The work you do on research methods and ethics is all part of this. You learn to interrogate context. When you work in a business you also need to understand the needs of the business because sometimes the business actually has directed a project, and you have to be at least you're aware of those needs. In my case also working in the technology sector, you also understand the limitations of technology and actually try to essentially marry those three (people, business and technological capacity) in a very distinct way. I think the MBA allowed me to know how business speaks and how business tries to build products that essentially extend its value. But I think the PhD, more than anything, really just gave me the credentials that gave me a voice inside the company and projects.

I'd like to move this conversation in a slightly different direction and say, as a black man in America, I am very aware of the politics of race in the United States and I feel that having a PhD allows me the platform to speak my truth. Not just that, it allows me to demand to be listened to and be able to position myself as an expert in my domain, however narrowed that domain is. I think it gives me access to the audience and allows people to actually listen to what I have to say. So that's quite useful because then, when people listen to you, you can then essentially advocate for things that otherwise are usually left out of the conversation. You advocate for those that are not present in the room, you advocate for those that are often othered and be able to speak to 'power' in this project sense. From a business standpoint, the potential benefits of including or bringing those that are often left out of discussions about projects, their developments and outcomes into the process.

Laurene: Thank you. That is a really interesting point because it is intimately connected to the PhD obviously, because it's about you and I suppose that's what I'm really interested in. This element of you and the idea of practice [are] always evolving – we are all in a perpetual state of improving practice and that's why it's both a verb and a noun. The whole self is in a practice and it's different to a project, which can be a thing. So thank you for sharing that because perhaps it's both a strategic, an intentional and an unintentional outcome or consequence of doing what is ostensibly the highest degree that you can do and one that is focused on building research expertise. You have reached that point. Was that your intention at the commencement of the PhD or is that something that you have discovered as you went through it and that you're finding more that you get to manifest now in your practice?

Dimeji: To speak as plainly as possible. While I was running my design practice, I found myself running in circles and I was finding myself thinking less about design and more about earning a living and paying bills and paying wages. I felt that I was more intentional about the MBA than I was about the PhD because I was hoping that the MBA was going to provide me with the networking and the perspectives that I needed to be able to advance my practice. I felt like the PhD was a little bit different because it allowed me to explore the things I cared about. I felt that it gave me the space to think about these issues and then to start thinking about how to engage with them.

I think most of that came as a realization later on. Now that I've earned a PhD, I have found that there are very few people in my position – you know, black and male in the United States with a PhD in design. I found that there are very few of those and I felt that that allowed me to be able to be in spaces and engage with others, either through mentorship or be able to speak in places and add value to the conversation and talk about perspectives that I had not often thought about. It was something that essentially came to me as a realization over time.

I think, if I had to phrase it differently, I feel that the PhD was somewhat intentional, but it was less intentional than the MBA. I think the realization came much later that there is a lot of responsibility that comes with having a PhD that you otherwise wouldn't have with a master's degree. Not only am I a practitioner. I am also always an academic and I have to continue to advance that practice and also push for critical thinking for designers.

Laurene: In your role at Google – do you mentor others within the teams that you work with or is your broader community the focus of this?

Dimeji: I mentor others within the team I work with as well as with the broader community. I give a number of talks within the company about these issues. I mentor younger designers within Google as well, and then I am also working with what they call 'employee resource groups' (ERGs). For example, when I was at Microsoft – I was a lead for the black ERG that sought to essentially make space for black designers in tech, what was called a 'retain lead', essentially trying to figure out how to make sure that black UXers stay in the company and they don't get burnt out. So yes, it's a responsibility.

One of the things I also realized within the tech industry is that depending on where you work, the PhD is often not as highly regarded as you see outside of tech. In a sense that many people don't really care whether or not you have a PhD, they just want to know that you can do the work. I think there is a little bit of that too, which is for good and bad. I'm curious to know what your thoughts are about that?

Laurene: Well, I think a reality is you don't need a degree to work as a designer, except in the fields that are accredited such as architecture or landscape architecture, and some areas of industrial design where it intersects with engineering or computer science. In many ways it is the difference between whether you can 'do' design or you have a design practice. Ideally a degree sets you up with a broader capacity and understanding of what design is and can contribute beyond the traditional areas of practice.

I think this is also the case with a design PhD programme, a PhD – and particularly one through practice or by project – is an opportunity for a practitioner to continue to explore of the fundamental pedagogic model of their undergraduate studies (where actions and outcomes of practice are deemed to be new knowledge), but you are required to evidence much deeper and informed practice than earlier studies.

So in that way a designer who undertakes a design PhD through design will find a lot of the things are actually consistent with their earlier studies. However designers might also have a PhD from any other area such as design management PhD or anthropology, they might have it in a quite different field and have deep knowledge of something outside of design, and despite this, there should be shared doctoral level research skills that are consistent. The PhD is the most advanced research-training degree, so it's about the competencies or the transferable knowledge, the capacity to do critical thinking, to design research studies, develop methods and understand ethics and the implications in projects. In other words, have the skills set to practice as a researcher.

I always tell students – the fact that you know a lot about the content of your PhD is great but that's got a really limited application. The reason organizations hire a PhD is because they have advanced research skills that can be applied to a topic. It's funny, I remember from my own PhD and from students I've supervised, often there's a point where you go really narrow and you think you know everything about your topic and then there's a point where you go, 'I don't know very much at all, but I know a lot about this bit, and I know what I don't know, and I know how I could know it.' That's kind of the 'doctoral moment' it is when you know what you know, you know what you don't and you know you can work out to know what you don't know with the same integrity.

Dimeji: Yes. If I could add something to that, you said that there's something about a PhD holder that they should be able to interrogate and I feel like there's, in practice, also another requirement that I would want to add to that is, really being able to translate ideas to make them more meaningful. A PhD holder must find a way to essentially tell that story in a way that their peers and those that they work with in practice get it and understand. I feel like unfortunately, we're in the age of fast design and everyone wants to make a decision quickly. No one is going to wait for you to do that thorough, durable research that you need to do and they are just going to keep moving and making decisions nonetheless.

One of the things that I feel a PhD should allow you to do is to find a way to tell that story in a way that people get it. I find myself in rooms sometimes sharing some ideas with peers and I just see the glazed-over look and at that moment, I realize that I have lost the audience. It's quite unfortunate, I know, but I have had to learn the skill of taking that knowledge and the connections that I have been able to make and the skill of making connections that I have learned and using that skill in a way that I can actually tell a story that people get and that aligns with their understanding. I feel like that is something that I quickly realized is a benefit of having a PhD in practice.

Laurene: Has that been one of the challenges for you? It's only three years since you graduated, and for the first year after a PhD you're usually pretty brain fogged and tired anyway – but is this ability to work at speed and communicate ideas something that you are working on?

Dimeji: I think I have gotten a lot better at it. I was fortunate, before I graduated with my PhD, I was already doing consultant work. I had already learnt to think quickly on my feet and think about what is relevant and how to share it. I have learnt to, where needed, to avoid jargon because people will not get it and what it means. Sometimes you just have to keep the jargon and I actually insist, you have to pick your battles, and say we are going to use this phrase because this phrase encapsulates the meaning of what I am trying to share in a more poignant way than any other phrase would.

Most times, you just have to let go of the jargon and find other ways to tell the story. I think I have learnt that and quite quickly too, because it really is a survival instinct, or strategy, to make sure that the people that you are working with get what you're sharing with them and I'm always careful to introduce theories. One thing I have learned about practice is also that people have latched onto certain things, and it's also being circulated all the way up the chain and so, it's very hard to essentially teach old dogs new tricks, so you have to pick your battles very carefully, know what is important to push for and what can be done differently.

You think about things like the hierarchy of needs, the product design space or product making space, it's like everyone has drunk the Kool-Aid and everybody believes that the 'holy grail' that you design for functional needs before you design it for aspirational needs. Initially, when I joined Microsoft, I was saying, 'Can we think about needs differently?' and I realized that no one was listening to me until we had to present to an executive-level leader. I sat in the meeting, and they were talking in terms of the hierarchy of needs and I quickly realized, 'Wait, there's no way we're going to think differently about this idea because it's already gone all the way up and everybody thinks this way!' So, you have to be careful and know the context that you are working and with who. You have to start with where they are and then you have to add into it and say, 'Well, yes. I understand that we think of it this way, but can we add "this" to it?' It almost has to be a subversive approach in certain ways, almost like a Trojan horse. You have to present something as though it's something else and then change it while they're not paying attention!

Laurene: I think that's a good analogy. I think designers always do that as Dan Hill argues in his book *Dark Matter* (2015).

What you are highlighting is consistent with what you do in PhD research. Originally, a PhD was understood as being an investigation into something new that had never been researched before, which we know is just not possible anymore with the amount of knowledge production, globally. Now doctoral research is understood to be an iteration or a particular application of discoveries in context. There continues to be an expectation of novelty and newness, but it is an incremental newness that is grounded and situated in the field or place. So, what you're reflecting on as an approach to introducing innovation or alternate perspectives into projects. You know what the parameters are and then you're trying to extend that and wonder how we can take it somewhere else. This of course happens in a lot of design practice, but it seems that the methods and strategies that you had to develop through doing the extended research of the PhD have supported you in being more strategic than you were before.

Dimeji: Thank you. I think learning how to make a contribution for greater good should be an essential part of doing a PhD in practice for practice. We talk about it in academia, what is the contribution to knowledge that this research is making? If you find yourself in professional practice, you also need to think in terms of this. If I were to leave this company I'm working at, what would I have added that might have changed certain parts of how the company thinks about their business? Because that's why I'm there. I tend to be very idealistic in certain ways about things but I really feel like we have a purpose there. We're trying to create or design change – and even if it's on a small scale that's fine too – but we're trying to essentially subvert the way business is done and do it in a careful way and that we're hopefully able to measure the successes that come from this.

Laurene: Is there anything that you wanted to tell me about your experience in retrospect?

Dimeji: I feel like it was really quite difficult at the very end. I had a consultancy project straight after completing the PhD programme – but I had been applying for academic work right after I finished as well, and I didn't get any. There is a cycle and there are a certain number of applications you can put out, a certain number of interviews you can do – and I wasn't getting accepted by any place. I was struggling with finding a job. I remember really, really struggling with that. I put out hundreds of applications. I was like an application making machine and I was just putting them out and I never really got an opportunity.

It wasn't until I had to self-reflect about what was happening, and I quickly realized that I never wanted to be in academia full time anyway. It wasn't something that was on my mind from the very beginning. From the very beginning I felt I was going to be working in practice and I was going to be a practitioner and I had to terms with that and say, 'you know what, my work is relevant for design practitioners, and I have to find a way to get back to that'. It wasn't until I did that that I realized that there was a place for me in practice and then I started getting calls from academic institutions!

Laurene: Was it while you were doing the PhD that you began to think that perhaps the logical path was to go into academia rather than practice? Did being part of the university context and the bigger narrative around PhDs and research that made you think that?

Dimeji: Yeah, I felt so. I felt that that was going to be the way. I would feel accepted, by my peers, if I was working in academia. I had to come to terms with the fact that I really don't give a damn what my peers think. I had my own reason for why I did the PhD, and I really had to essentially go and pursue that, as opposed to finding acceptance in academia. I think initially, I was thinking to myself, all the folks in my cohort were getting jobs as professors and I felt like I needed to go get a job as a professor but in reality it wasn't for me.

I do teach in different universities now, but I teach the courses I want to teach. I make the courses – I write the courses – and I work with the school to essentially push those courses forward. Those are not courses that are normally taught within the academic institution, and I think I feel a lot better contributing this way because it allows me to still push innovations without consequences. I'm able to be force around the topics I care about.

I do think that if we had had this conversation three years ago, I would probably be a really miserable guy, feeling like the PhD was all a waste but now, I think it all worked out because this was how it was meant to evolve, and this is exactly what I was meant to be doing. I have come to terms with working with a PhD within a tech company because I feel like some of the ideas that I have been sharing would not have gone out if I had not worked in a company with this much visibility. I feel like it's all working out.

Laurene: Are there many other PhDs in the business that you encounter?

Dimeji: Quite a few in my space, but PhDs with different backgrounds. So, folks in sociology, linguistics, clinical psychology and math. I work with lots of PhDs but very few in design.

Laurene: Do you feel a synergy with the other PhDs, though?

Dimeji: I feel there's mutual respect. You know that we all went through the ringer and that everybody understands what it meant to have earned one. If we are working together, there is a mutual level of expectation of the rigour of the research or the design explorations we are going to be doing, so that is expected. But I feel like outside of that, I think there's very little synergy in that sense. We just all understand the discipline that undertaking a PhD has taught us and we all know that. There's also an expectation that to remember that discipline is to apply it and we've all been carefully applying that rigour to the work.

Laurene: That's actually a very interesting place for me. You've raised some interesting points for me in terms of this research and the premise of the book. I'm not really looking for commonalities across the different discussions with the different people in the book, rather the themes that I have observed in my own students' experiences.

I think it's about both the agency of the PhD, which seems to be the authority it gives you because of the recognition of the PhD, and the calibre of what you have done to be awarded one, but also, how some of the methodologies, the manoeuvres you learn through doing the research that you are able to translate into everyday practice as well. I think that is very interesting because sometimes, people think that PhDs are about researching something that is really focused that can either be applied or not. What you've been talking about today shows that this has not been the case for you. You've shared a suite of competencies that you can use every day with peers, with your colleagues and also understanding how to have that practice that is always evolving.

Dimeji: I think what I want to add, that is somewhat related I think, if someone is contemplating doing one, they should also think about the folks with whom you do the PhD. Your cohort really matters because it's a very particular kind of learning moment. That has been a huge benefit for me, and I continue to stay connected with my cohort. I have worked on projects with different members of the group I did the PhD with and we invite one another to speak at classes for those that are teaching. I have someone that we have regular biweekly calls to talk about projects that we want to do together or just to check in.

I think that's, for me, one of the great benefits of doing it is you know the folks you did the PhD with, and I think you carry that with you for the rest of your life.

Laurene: It is a long and intense relationship – also, with your advisers. It is a special community because you go through it together. It seems to be really essential at the end of the study when no one else in your life understands the challenges you're having trying to finish the dissertation and you're going insane because you just can't get a chapter to work, no one else in your life actually understands that insanity and that focus. Some research shows that the PhD can be the loneliest study experience because of the length of individual project focus. Being part of a vibrant and connected community is essential.

Dimeji: You go through the ringer with a few folks and it's almost like you have battle scars to tell the story. I think, to a certain extent, that is the way it is. That's why, when you see another PhD in practice – someone with a PhD in practice – you don't really care so much about what their topic of inquiry was, most of them are just the fact that they've got a PhD and they went through that process, and you respect that.

Portrait of Daria Loi

4

Trusting in the process

Laurene Vaughan speaks with Daria Loi

Dr Daria Loi has had an adventurous career and education trajectory. She has traversed fields of study, domains of practice and a range of professional roles. She is a researcher and leader in participatory design and an advocate for people and their experiences. Recently she has focused her leadership in workplace well-being and professional interactions in the design and technology sectors.

In the following conversation, Daria reflects on her experience of doctoral studies, and the challenges and strategies that she devised to complete her studies. Cross-disciplinarity, interdisciplinarity and disciplinary differences were fundamental to her research and her subsequent career development. Much published discourse focuses on the outcomes of doctoral enquiry and what a person comes to know about 'something', but Daria emphasizes the importance of process in terms of research, design and practice orientation. Being committed to the process of the research and holding fast to that (even as great challenges and blocks were encountered) allowed for new learnings, innovations and, possibly most significantly, resilience to emerge.

There are two aspects to the resilience that Daria developed through her PhD experience: personal strategic resilience and intellectual resilience. Both were underpinned by trust: trust in herself, her openness and integrity, and trust in process. We cannot know the outcomes, even if pursuing a hunch, an idea or a passion; we must set the wheels in motion and keep moving with the project.

The term 'soft skills' comes up in the conversation, and how important interpersonal and communication skills are. Daria reflects on the impact of the challenges she faced in her studies – the misunderstandings, biases and ultimately the relocation of her research to a supervisor and context that was brave and interested in what she was endeavouring to do. These challenges provided her with soft skills that she has gone on to refine in her different professional roles and contributions. But these skills are anything but soft; they are wily and subtle and take time to refine. They demand listening and observational expertise, and an interest in those that you are working and/or communicating with. It is fascinating to hear how Daria has refined and applied this capacity in her roles in user experience, ethnographic fieldwork and working across disciplinary teams. The outcome is an ongoing fascination about people and how design can serve them.

Impactful leaders in any field must be lifelong learners. They know what they know and what they don't know. They seek out information, communities, mentors and contexts to continue to grow, and through this growth be capable of meaningful leadership. In Daria's case, she shares the way in which her doctoral studies and her experience of doing the PhD enabled her to develop this capacity in her roles, practice and the doctoral submission itself.

In the following conversation, Daria speaks to her experience of challenging the academic norms of what a *thesis* should be as a material artefact. In the end she submits her PhD thesis in the form of a suitcase (Figures 4.1–4.3).

Laurene: Thank you for participating in this research. To my mind, you have had an interesting career trajectory. You were a designer and then an academic, completed a PhD and then returned to practice. So perhaps if we could commence with you sharing, how you went from being in practice and teaching to then doing the PhD, what your PhD was in and what format and field it was in.

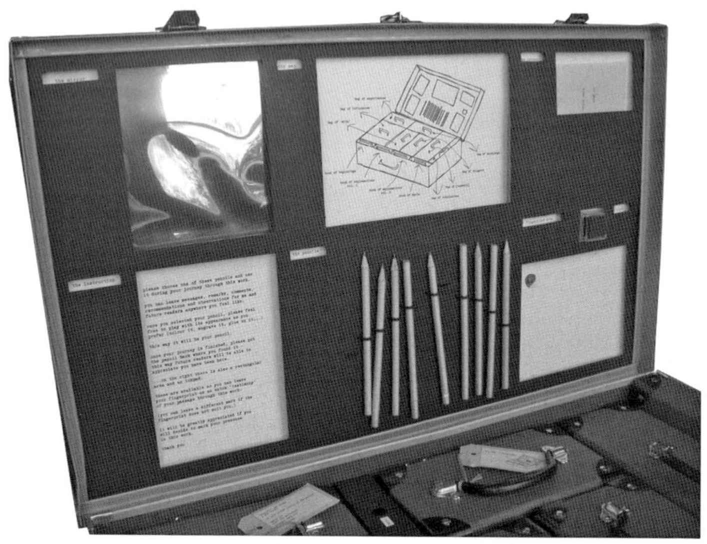

FIGURE 4.1 *Daria Loi, Suitcase.*

Daria: I think that a timeline might help. I originally
studied architecture in Italy. However, after experiencing
architecture life in a studio, I concluded that the profession
was not for me, so I moved to Australia to do a graduate
course. I wanted to expand my knowledge, bring learnings
back and start a different design practice. I never intended to
be an academic, but things changed as I was offered a role in
the same department where I was conducting my PhD.

When I started my graduate studies, I thought, 'I'll
learn, do field work on collaborative spaces and write
it all up. I'll get a rubber stamp and become a design

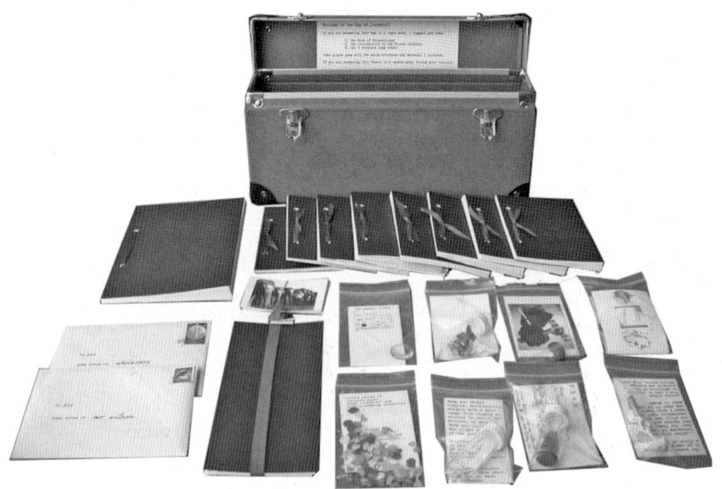

FIGURE 4.2 *Daria Loi, Bag Answers.*

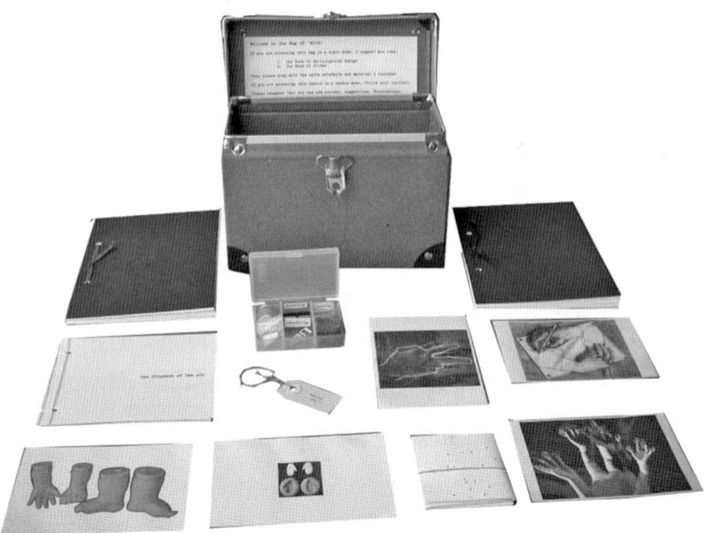

FIGURE 4.3 *Daria Loi, Bag Influences.*

practitioner in this new field. Voilà.' Instead, while the intent was solely to study collaborative spaces, I ended up learning something more important: the limitation of my own practice.

Somehow, I was under the delusion – a delusion that many designers seem to have – that from my designer ivory tower I'd be able to envision the ultimate collaborative space. Somehow my golden designer touch would create a space that would make its users compelled to collaborate. Instead, I ended up realizing that if people do not wish to collaborate, the space is not going to do much, regardless of how masterfully it is designed. A space can support, but cannot create collaboration.

Suddenly it became very evident that design – the design that interested me – was not what I initially understood and studied. I realized that I needed to shift from designing things to designing experiences. That was when I started becoming who I am today. That was THE moment – and with that, the PhD also evolved. My role was not to design a space – it was to leverage design tools to create collaborative dynamics among teams and individuals and then facilitate their workspace co-design. First facilitate collaboration, then facilitate collaborative spaces co-design. The designed artefact – the workspace – was not the beginning and centre at all. The experience was.

While writing the new PhD, it became evident that I couldn't submit a normal thesis format. I felt that there was a hard-to-ignore dichotomy between me advocating for participatory practices and me articulating content in a format (thesis manuscript) that gives little to no agency to its end users (readers). I still wanted to submit a thesis yet a different kind, an alternative thesis format. However, the process for that did not exist back then and had to fight pretty hard to get a go-ahead. That said, after much persistence and perseverance, the university eventually allowed me to submit the format I felt most appropriate. My question was, 'How can I engage the users (readers) of this object (thesis) so they can engage with it in the same participatory ways that I'm advocating for in the thesis?' It was a babushka doll question if you like.

Interestingly enough, the alternative PhD format was what opened the serendipitous door for my going back to non-academic work and move to the US. This story starts with me reading a Canadian academic's blog referencing my unusual PhD and how she learned about it from an anthropologist at Intel. I recall feeling so curious . . . *how did someone in such a large company learn about my work? An anthropologist in a corporation?* Curiosity is what prompted me to write to the anthropologist, 'Can we have a chat? I'd like to learn why you think my work is interesting to you, given your context.'

This story is important for our conversation, as the non-traditional competencies that I acquired during that somewhat painful and unusual PhD journey ended up being representative of what this company was trying to hire. They had a gap in knowledge and my non-standard design knowledge and experience was considered a valuable asset.

I accepted the job, moved to the USA and had a plan: learn and take learnings back to academia. But then I kept on thinking, 'There's a little bit more to learn.' So, here I am, fifteen years later – I don't think I will ever fully return to academia. That said, I never stopped engaging with academia as there are so many opportunities to be connected from the outside.

Laurene: That's interesting because I think there are two things I'd like to pick up on: firstly, what are these competencies that you feel that these new traditional, new-old design competencies that emerged through the PhD, and then secondly how do you integrate your two contexts of contribution – practice and academia? You're still very much part of the academic community and very much part of a research community, whilst as you say, not being employed within academia. This may be in some ways particular to the field of design you work in. But it's a very research-led field of practice I would describe it. I'd be interested to know what you think about this integration of contexts.

Daria: Yes, absolutely. So, the first part is the competencies. . . . I might go on a few tangents as I do not have a list written up . . .

Laurene: That's fine.

Daria: I will share not in hierarchical order, but as they come to my mind. First, I think that designers often overfocus on the idea of design as an outcome and frequently confuse their design mastery with their creations. Through the PhD journey I've come to appreciate something that I bring to my job daily: design competency has nothing to do with outcomes. The real competency is the process. That's all there is to it. The process. When I think about the value that I brought to organizations over the years, the ability to focus on process and unfold complexity through that process is what comes to mind as key competency.

This takes me to a second competency. During my journey supervisors and fellow travellers kept telling me that in a PhD, 'you dig deep to become a master of one thing. You keep on excavating – deeper, deeper and deeper.' But you see, I was a bit rebellious and kept questioning, 'There's a lot of things around here on the side that are so interesting! Why are you telling me to go down there? I don't want to go there. I want to connect, not specialize in one thing.' I now believe that being that rebellious, in some ways, paid off. The ability to go deep yet not in one single specialized direction and the tenacity of saying, 'No, let me look at the world from 10,000 miles and let me see how things connect – what connects to what, even when things seem to different,' served me well.

Being able to identify, understand and appreciate diverse trajectories and connections . . . being able to tie together seemingly different data points and voices to create a new story in which those connections matter and play a lead role in creating a new product, service or system that is meaningful. . . . That ability of seeing that interconnectedness inside complex contexts, problem areas, opportunities. . . . If I had to extract the core thing that I do, love doing or attempt to do every day in my job – that would be it. It's a *designerly* way of looking at the world, making sense and connecting dots – dots that to a designer may feel obvious, or even visible, but that in fact are not to stakeholders, clients or collaborators.

Arguably, with some purposeful training one could acquire this ability and in the context of my specific architectural studies I have to admit that we were shaped to think that way. Yet, while I recognize that trajectory in my bachelor upbringing, I strongly believe that the PhD, my specific way of experiencing the PhD, was what made me see things that way and what made me resilient.

This now takes us to a third competency: the ability to be resilient, determined and focused. During the PhD

I experienced so many moments where I wanted to give up – the process at times was painful, confusing and demoralizing. I wanted to give up yet I did not. And the process of not giving up gave me an ability that is key and an everyday necessity in industrial contexts. Resilience, determination, focus, but also being . . . 'opportunistic'? . . . not the right word because it sounds negative . . .

Laurene: Strategic?

Daria: Maybe strategic, thank you. That's better. Keep your goals in the forefront; don't listen to the NOs and naysayers – unless of course you deep down feel that you should. I recall a time when I wrote a paper and really wanted to present it at a conference that accepted it – but I didn't have enough money to travel. I asked for funding because I felt the paper was important but the Head of the Department gave me a solid NO as an answer. So, I proceeded writing to the Head of School, who replied something on the lines of 'If you find someone else that gives you some money for this, I'll match it.' I guess the idea was that I'd never get it. So, I wrote to the Vice Chancellor, 'Here is my journey and why I need to go to this conference. I think this paper is important, but I don't have money. I'm a full-time international student and I'm working full time to pay for my PhD fees. I have no money; can you help please? The Head of School told me that she will match whatever funding I can get from elsewhere. Will you give me something, so she'll match it?' To my surprise, she replied, 'Sure, I will.'

People thought I was nuts when I did this, yet that determination and focus and ability to say, 'No, I do believe this is the right thing to do and I'm not going to listen to you telling me that this is not achievable, because this is important, and I'm going to go and get it' paid off in the end. So that is an example of the type of pressure the PhD put on me. I'm not saying that I'm advocating for students to experience that pressure, by the way, in any possible way! Yet I think that the pressure helped me acquire soft skills and competencies that one does not get from a course or book. Experiencing difficulties, confronting challenges, not accepting NOs, moving forward despite all odds, picking myself up and learning by doing is what helped me.

Those 'soft' skills, as they are often referred to, were fundamental and I observe myself applying them all the time. One could say that I can be completely shameless but honestly, I've learned during that time that the worst that can happen when you ask for something is a 'no'. So, who cares? Literally, that's a key lesson I've learned during my PhD: the worst that can happen to you when you ask for something because you need help is that someone will say 'no', and that 'no' has more to do with the person that says no than it has with you. And that's the end of that.

I always share this simple learning with mentees, employees . . . even friends and family. I ask, 'What do you have to lose if you try? Nothing? Well then, why don't you do it? Just go and try. Do not worry about making mistakes but please avoid not trying just because you're scared of getting a no.'

I learned a lot of key and hard lessons during my PhD. It was painful yet great learning. It shaped me. Ultimately, despite a few humiliations, many NOs and disappointments, multiple backstabbing and the occasional yet blatant BS . . . despite it all, I kept moving forward and kept telling myself, 'I'm going to keep pushing because there's a story worth telling.' In the workplace as in life, we all have to deal with naysayers; people that are unkind or unsupportive; that disagree without solid reason; that sabotage our vision or curb our enthusiasm; people that exclude instead of including. We all have to face party poopers. That's how work life works. That's life.

These life skills, soft skills, are super important. When I interview people for jobs, that is a key thing that people seem to lack, underestimate or forget to highlight. Candidates come with amazing degrees, amazing portfolios, blah, blah, and then you ask three or four questions about life skills and you're like, 'No. I cannot have you in my team, thank you.' This is something that I hope academia will focus on with great emphasis: teaching soft skills. They are so key to one's success. A second skill that I wish for academia to teach more cohesively and comprehensively to strengthen the future workforce is systemic thinking – the ability of seeing connections. A third one is the ability for designers to understand that they can (and should be able to) design anything – the process is the key and that can be applied to anything: how one manages people; creates a marketing vision; designs a car; conducts oneself in life; conceives an idea; develops a policy; talks and writes.

When I reflect on the strategic, systemic thinking capability, I distinctively recall a moment while writing my PhD's methodology chapter. I dreaded it because I was trying so hard to write it in what I perceived to be the 'right way of writing a methodology chapter'. It was awful. I was like, 'I hate this.' I just could not do it.

Then at one point, I thought, 'Screw this, I don't care', and I threw everything in the rubbish bin. I started again. I was like, 'I'm going to do what I think is right and if my supervisor tells me, it's rubbish, I will start again, but I'm going to throw this one away. I'm going to start from scratch.' As soon as I let that go – that weight of trying to be what you think others want you to be – things changed. As designers, quite often, we forget that we are meant to think outside the box – I certainly forgot it when I wrote the first version of that chapter. Seeing things differently is a key value that as designers we bring yet sometimes it gets lost, especially when there seems to be a 'right way' and a 'wrong way' of doing things. Instead of fitting into a predefined mould, the designer should think, 'Hold on, I'm a designer! I do not have to be that way.'

And that is what I did. All of a sudden, I was like, 'Why am I trying to fit? I'm supposed to be a designer. I'm supposed to look at problems in a different way and that's the value I should be able to bring. So let me do this, and if it's wrong, you can tell me later, and I'll move on.' It felt wonderful to suddenly have that realization and the ability of letting go of the noise, looking at myself from the outside, out of pre-packaged standardized bubbles, and reflect, 'Is this really the only way in which we can look at this problem?'

This is the same dynamic that may happen when designers practice their craft: you're in front of a problem and you stare at it so long that you start forgetting that there may be many ways of looking at that problem. You keep focusing in one direction and, the moment you do that, everything gets narrower, and you're trapped. But as a designer you have the opportunity and authorization to stop, slow down, look at the issue from multiple viewpoints, explore and only then settle for a range of possible solutions.

To me, that moment in the methodology chapter was like that. I rushed and settled for one direction that I perceived to be the recommended 'right way' – and the more I went on, the more it became torture. I was trapped by my own web. But then I stepped back, and it was like, 'Ha-ha!' This is actually what I often do at work. I am in a meeting room with engineers and programme managers, and I hear myself saying, 'Have we looked at the problem from diverse perspectives? Do we have all the data, from diverse viewpoints? Was this the right problem to focus on in the first place?'

That ability of slowing down, stepping back, looking at things, asking hard question and reflecting on them . . . it is a capability that some may have naturally but, in my case, I don't believe so. It is something that I continuously work on. It's a lifelong journey, let's put it this way. From that perspective the PhD was a huge stepping stone for me. Very formative.

Laurene: Yes, it does, and I think it's interesting. I don't want to put my assumptions or perspective on your experience. But as you're speaking, I'm wondering if the fact that you did your PhD in management and not in design . . .

Daria: No, it actually started as industrial design.

Laurene: So, you started in industrial design and then you moved to . . .

Daria: Management, because of my supervisor.

Laurene: I'm just wondering – do you think that being in that different context, a different cultural context of knowledge production, of epistemology, how we evaluate what's valid, even knowing that qualitative research potentially at that time was still slightly contested. Action learning and research was still having to be justified. Do you think that having to go outside of your disciplinary comfort zone and your known language influenced your experience and the outcomes?

Daria: Yes, absolutely, 100 per cent yes. Interestingly enough, once I moved to that department, it was much easier. I actually found that context – not management in general, but that supervisor in that specific department – open minded, understanding of what I was trying to do, open to my vision. . . . I have a story about this. It's pretty funny, in the end.

When I decided my alternative PhD-suitcase format, the department suggested I submitted a PhD by project I was like, 'No, this is a thesis. You are misunderstanding the intent of my work.' My supervisor supported me but the department's research committee was like, 'We have only two processes for submission: by thesis and by project. We don't have a thing that is by thesis but is not a book. It doesn't fit. We're not against it, but you don't fit. We don't know where to put you.' So, they told me, 'Why don't you do a prototype, and you present to the research committee of the management faculty?'

So here I am with my suitcase prototype in front of the committee. I do my roadshow, they asked me questions. It's all great, except that the feedback is something like, 'We think it's a great idea, but we feel uncomfortable to give you the go-ahead. Why don't you go to the university research committee?' So here I am with my suitcase prototype in front of another committee. It was the most bizarre situation: a board room with one or two representatives for every faculty – diverse set of disciplines, including the two creative faculties, Architecture & Design, and Communication. I immediately assumed that those creative representatives would be more open to my case, 'The hard one is going to be all the others . . . engineering . . . all the quantitative driven faculties.' Well, believe it or not, the only two people in the entire room that were against were the two people from the creative faculties but because the majority said yes, they were like, 'Meh'. So, in the end I received a letter – this is the funniest thing – giving me the go-ahead, but with an addendum stating that the university would 'not take any responsibility if the PhD failed'.

Laurene: Washing their hands off it.

Daria: Washing their hands. I'm like, 'Okay, I don't care. I'm
going to do my thing.' I did and submitted. After reviewers
sent their evaluation back, I received a phone call from
the Head of the Research Committee, the person that
managed the entire process including suitcase roadshow
and letter, to congratulate me because he never received
a unanimous 100 per cent with no changes required and
such positive feedback from both the examiners. All
those people, that for so long tried to stop my submission,
suddenly, were ecstatic for my and the university's success.
'Mm, okay? Thank you. I'm glad that you're glad for
me. But you tried to . . .' Oh well, okay . . . this was an
interesting part of the journey, and a key lesson was to not
make assumptions on who is or is not friendly only due to
disciplinary association.

Going back to your comment about comfort zones. . . .
When I changed supervisors and had to move the PhD to
the management department, two aspects turned out to be
extremely formative learning opportunities. First, as you
suggested, moving out of my comfort zone forced me to be
even more crystal clear about my design messaging because
. . . here I am in a faculty, in a school, of non-designers. I had
to adapt and that is a competency that I leverage all the time
now – being able to adapt, to keep the core of a story intact,

but to adapt how I tell that story, depending on the audience. I have to do it at work all the time.

Suddenly, I was in the management field and had to embrace a completely different literature and way of seeing the world. I had to stretch myself in a very different direction. It was a valuable lesson, which influenced me in many ways, including how I manage people. Also, I couldn't talk about my practice in the same way, as I had to explain my work to non-designers – I could not make the same assumptions or use the same lingo.

The second formative aspect was that my main supervisor was almost completely blind. There I was, a designer with a three-dimensional object that includes a lot of visuals, explaining it all with words. That is when I learned how to translate the essence without losing the meaning. How to make things visual without visuals. That is again about adapting to those in front of you – it's about trying to understand where they're coming from, their language, their culture and their disciplinary assumptions. You cannot project your own assumptions and instead you need to give space and have a conversation.

That skills ended up being super valuable. When I am in meetings and people can't find a way to talk to each other, I can use it to mediate. When I have user data that needs to be heard, I can use it to ensure engineers understand and act on it. This capability of abstracting and translating became fundamental. Without it I probably would not have been able to finish my PhD.

So absolutely, you're right. My move to another discipline was key, as was cross-disciplinary work. During that time, to pay my international student fees I applied and was granted a scholarship that required cross-disciplinary work. I learned so much during that experience – it was such a stellar opportunity which I wish was given to all students. Now, I think the other thing you were wanting to talk about had more to do with academia.

Laurene: Well, I was interested in how is it academia or is a research community that you're actively involved with? I suppose that would be my question, but I know that you publish; you do a lot of presentations; you're very engaged in a range of ways. So, I'm wondering the PhD may have well been the introduction into that community, but I'm interested as a practitioner within such a community, how do you find that?

Daria: I find academia endlessly fascinating. First of all, there is always something to learn from a given community and in academia there are many people that I admire, you being one of them. Many thought leaders. I think that that's how one grows, by learning through others and thanks to others. Second, academic thinking has something that industry thinking doesn't: the luxury of time. Academia operates on very different timelines: you can investigate a topic for years or several months – a luxury that you typically don't have in industry. Being able to reflect on things, go deeper and even have the time to put it all down in academic writing. . . . There's something very valuable in that. I love academic reading, writing and thinking. I find it all very enriching and formative. I can engage with it and then abstract and translate what I learned in ways that make sense in my own non-academic context.

Third, I love engaging with academia because of the students – the aspect that I miss the most about my academic career. Usually when I'm asked to give lectures to students, I cannot say no. Literally, I am incapable. When a student reaches out and says, 'Can you read my paper?' I'm like, 'Okay'. I really find it hard to say no to students because (a) I find them exciting, (b) I want to give back the good things that I received when I was a student. Students are full of life, oomph and creativity – they enrich me.

Fourth, the act of writing and sharing with others your work is so crucial. Throughout my PhD as well as my prior thesis at Politecnico di Milano, I came to appreciate that when you're forced to put down in writing complex ideas, you have the opportunity to crystalize what you really learnt and mean. In industry, we do stuff, yet that act of articulating things within a constrained wordcount and in ways that others can fully understand yet academically forces you to crystalize what you know, what matters and what you learned. It is powerful and I love doing that. I also love presenting and sharing with others – I get a lot of energy from that as it makes me feel connected with other humans.

Now, you asked me about my engagement with academia and the reality is that I don't see myself as 100 per cent industry now, as I did not see myself as 100 per cent academic when I was in academia. Here's a story that talks of that. When I was a PhD student, I and a couple colleagues presented to a big-shot professor the value of hybridizing one's practice through cross-disciplinarity. We felt that it was going to become a key competency for future workers. I remember him shutting us down pretty harshly, providing the feedback that our proposal was absolutely ludicrous and suggesting that we were damaging ourselves and our careers by engaging in hybridization. He said that 'You're going to be neither this nor that.' Ironically, we ended up writing a paper about it. More ironically, years later the same professor became a strong advocate of cross-disciplinarity. I shared this story of hybridization as I've always seen myself as a hybrid between industry and academia. The space between those two is very valuable to me.

I must however admit that when I am in academic contexts, like academic conferences, sometimes it's frustrating. For example, when I invite academics to share their great work to industry, I often find myself thinking, 'This is wonderful work' but 'Why didn't they cater the presentation to this audience? Why aren't they explaining themself in ways that this audience can understand, appreciate and use?' Similarly, when leaders from big-shot big corporations present in an academic context, I am often thinking, 'Oh come on . . . Don't say that! They won't listen to you if you articulate your work that way. Your work is so good, yet you don't know how to talk about it here. Change your lingo and attitude!' As a hybrid I understand and appreciate both sides, but I often realize this may not be the norm. I wish there were more hybrids. There is so much that academia could learn from the industry and there's so much that the industry could learn from academia. The two sides don't speak the same language, and, because of that, they don't even try to listen to each other. It's so painful to observe.

As a hybrid, I am compelled to connect and communicate with different audiences and that ability is helpful in reaching the goals I set for myself. I keep the key message and goal in the forefront and adapt the rest. So, for example, if my goal is to ensure inclusion of a key capability in a product because end users shared it is crucial for them – in other words if my goal is to ensure that the product is a good one for users – then I'm not going to waste my time with semantic, abstractions or disciplinary purity. I keep the goal's purity in the forefront and adapt the rest.

When I moved from an R&D department to a business unit in the same company, for example, many colleagues thought I was nuts. Back then, nobody wanted to work with that group because 'They don't listen to designers or researchers. They don't care about users. You're going to hate it'. I was the only design researcher in that team – the rest were engineers, strategy and marketing planners, and business executives. I was the only person that looked like me and I remember thinking, 'I'm going to pay attention to my audience. How do they talk? What do they care about?' I interviewed my new colleagues and stakeholders as if it was a field project and through that activity I came to see and appreciate what made them pause, listen and act. I started shaping my data collection and presentation strategy to be able to tell a story that would make them pause, listen and act. By playing across disciplines and contexts you can achieve so much more.

Laurene: It's quite challenging to do.

Daria: Yeah. Maybe because it's not a hard disciplinary competence per se and most disciplines overlook it because of that. Yet I believe that it's a key competency that one should have. There is a lot to be learned from academia as there is a lot to learn from industry and any other discipline that is not one's core background. In academia there is depth, critical thinking, reflective thinking – the industry so often forgets all that and it's so dangerous. Academia helps me avoid getting colonized by industry's somewhat superficial ways of thinking and doing. It helps me look at things from the outside, cultivate my ability to be a critical thinker, challenge and ask difficult questions.

Laurene: That's good. You've raised some interesting points that I think will be of great interest and value to others as you've gone through. It's really brought out the interdisciplinarity, the competencies and what they look like and how you bring them in your way. Thank you.

Portrait of Andrea Siodmok

5

Enacting curiosity

**Laurene Vaughan speaks with
Andrea Siodmok**

Throughout her career, Dr Andrea Siodmok OBE has adventured across and beyond conventional expectations of design practice and contributions and into new disciplinary collaborations. Andrea originally trained as an industrial designer, but found at the completion of her studies that she hadn't quite got to where she wanted to be. She was curious to have a deeper understanding of what design could do, and how, in collaboration with other disciplines, she could build a practice that would add value and challenge conventions. This curiosity has led her in an exciting career and ongoing learning journey.

In this conversation, she shares how the learnings made during and after her PhD provided the methods and rigour required to transition from a practice of making to one of advocacy and innovation. Andrea took time out from her doctoral studies to join the Design Council in the United Kingdom. This was a domain-changing time for design, with new fields of practice emerging and, notably, Tim Brown's (2009) term 'design thinking' gaining traction in business, policy and other sectors. Design was expanding, and the question of who designs was becoming far more complex than it had been when the focus was on the craft of design.

As Andrea reflects on her various roles, the organizations she has worked in and the people she collaborated with, it becomes apparent that the rigour of research training that a PhD demands is a good grounding for advocating design across disciplinary boundaries. Having worked and researched across a range of spheres, Andrea emphasizes the importance of understanding the context of practice and collaborations, and how building respectful, informed relationships is essential for this.

PhDs are often spoken of in relation to their outputs, the time they require, the examination process and post-PhD life. Each of these aspects is important, but the PhD is more than the sum of these. The sheer length and focus of the study, the individual nature of the research and the determination and innovations that a student must embrace to complete are all quite unique, and this conversation incorporates a theme of building resilience and tenacity. In this conversation, it is apparent that the curiosity that led Andrea into the PhD has stayed with her long after the doctorate was completed. Curiosity, as a disposition for discovery and building cross-disciplinary collaborations, seems to be a mainstay for her ongoing design practice.

Laurene: Perhaps we could commence with you sharing what was the catalyst for why you did your PhD?

Andrea: I had a curiosity. I had a question that I'd been developing through my undergraduate studies that I felt was a question that I had started to interrogate but hadn't completed. I also felt that the undergraduate course wasn't academic enough; it was very practice based and portfolio focused which was fine, but I felt I wanted to do something more or different. I'd done quite a lot of essays as well as the dissertation that was part of my undergraduate studies, and I just didn't feel like it had gone far enough in terms of difficulty. I wanted something a little bit more challenging that would be more theoretical to sit alongside the practice.

Laurene: Is that what you experienced in the PhD?

Andrea: Yes, I think it probably was and I probably shaped it that way. The studentship that I had was open ended regarding the topic of the study. It was for me to determine the topic that I wanted to study. Once I had done that, I then found a corporate research partner, who co-funded the study. This took a bit of time to put in place, but it meant that I had a free rein on how theoretical and how practical I wanted the PhD to be, and it was a mixture of both.

Laurene: With this ambition in mind, what do you think you learnt from doing the PhD, not necessarily regarding the research topic of the PhD but through doing the PhD?

Andrea: I was thinking about this the other day. I think there were definitely a number of things that I wouldn't be able to do now had I not undertaken the PhD. I think that the PhD gave a scaffolding to my practice in terms of a theoretical structure.

I think it enabled me to situate design practice in the context of both design theory but then also in the context of other research theories and other world views. Scientific world views and other methodologies really, so it gave me that methodological construct and language. I literally had just been making stuff prior to that point. I remember from when I was relatively new into my career, someone saying to me 'design is an iterative process'. I found this really curious, I was like, 'Is it?' I didn't know whether it was or wasn't because I'd never labelled it. I'd never intellectualized it. I'd just done it.

So, whether it was or wasn't iterative wouldn't have occurred to me or many of the undergraduates I studied with. Thinking about what is happening when you're designing was not something that we did a lot of. They do now, which is what I find quite curious. Having subsequently trademarked the Double Diamond methodology when I was at the Design Council, I now see that process being taught in a quite prescriptive way in academic settings. I wonder if that just takes away some of the freedom that up until that point of being told about this approach to designing, people were designing without form and structure expectations. That is a very long-winded way of saying it gave meaning to the context of the practice.

Laurene: When you finished your PhD what did you go on to do, what kind of job roles?

Andrea: I had been teaching alongside doing the PhD, so the PhD ended up being part time. I then went to the Design Council as their Research and Knowledge Manager and then became their Head of Design Knowledge before becoming the first Chief Design Officer. I had a design promotion job and put the PhD aside for a few years and worked full time. Eventually I came back to it and then completed it. Overall, it was very aligned in many ways to my interests with my teaching but also the research. I'd been teaching a design theory course alongside the PhD called Contemporary Influences on Design. It was about design ethics, design environment, inclusive design: all the different kind of theories of design that students needed to know.

I then moved to the Design Council to lead their research agenda. Initially we looked at the list of the topics I'd been teaching; we looked at the topics the Design Council wanted to have a viewpoint on, and they married up almost exactly. It was a very logical kind of link to demystifying design, promoting design, communicating the value of design. That all flowed very naturally from the PhD and from my teaching.

Laurene: Reflecting on how you've progressed throughout your career, I'm interested to talk about the influence that the PhD as an advanced research-training degree has had. You've talked today about your practice and the making. Then about the adaptation or application of your expertise and interests in what you've been teaching and into the Design Council work which I think we can call advocacy through such an organization. Do you think you could have done that work without the PhD?

Andrea: Technically I didn't have the PhD completed but I had gone through quite a lot of it.

I think your point about advocacy is a really important one and I suspect that's probably been a thread that's run through my career way beyond my time at the Design Council and I went on to use it in my work around design in government. I feel that a lot of my role has been 'field building' around pushing the boundaries of design and putting design into new contexts. But in order to do that I've needed to be able to understand the conceptual nature of the context that I'm moving design into. Most recently, that's why I did my Masters in Economics because I was working with economists and their world view was very different.

For me to be an effective advocate for design in the context of politics and economics, I needed to understand their construct and frameworks and the marrying of the two. So yes, I definitely leant very heavily on the PhD to do that job in communicating the value of design, demystifying it, because it felt much more concrete. I think having done that research and being able to verbalize the value of design has been essential.

I think it has been said before that design is distorted in its translation into words including promotion and things like that. It is changed by the practice of promoting it. So that whole point about when you advocate for design or when you describe design is that it kind of ceases to be design and becomes another form. Which maybe sounds a little bit esoteric but in reality, I think this has been my experience.

I suppose it's no different than trying to describe art or some other creative form that fundamentally is a different way of perceiving and of knowing. I think the PhD is the same. It takes a rather, sometimes difficult pathway between those worlds of practice and theory. I remember being told quite early in my journey that when you do a PhD in Design you do two PhDs. You do the practice and then you do the thesis, so you kind of do it twice and I could absolutely relate to that at the time.

Laurene: Yes, very common in the much earlier days of PhDs, I hope that it is becoming less so now.

I say that, but in reality it depends on where you are. There are still so many different forms of the design PhD, globally. This I think talks to what you are saying about the translation of design into different language forms when advocating for design. In doctoral education, or Design PhDs, people often had to do two PhDs because there was a fear about the rigour or 'doctoralness' of practice, the artefacts of practice and their processes. This led to the phenomenon that it was only through the theorizing or the application of somebody else's theory to the design that it gained the rigour that assured people of the integrity of the research work. Over the twenty-plus years I've been working in graduate research education I have observed that this has shifted, be it slowly. Perhaps in conjunction with the confidence that design has of itself, as a profession or a suite of disciplines, gained confidence and broader recognition.

Andrea: Yes, and we had this in the early stages of the RAE (the Research Assessment Exercise) in the UK. For example, in our studio in our research group, we had an individual who had designed Ducati motorbikes. On one level they were an amazing contribution to design practice and knowledge, but we found it really difficult to position them within the Research Assessment Exercise framework that required us to debate whether that practice had validity in its own right or whether it needed some other kind of external value ascribing to it in the way that you say.

In my PhD I leaned quite heavily on action research methods, for example, as a mechanism. I was examining a PhD last week, and I'm still seeing a lot of the pattern of what I wrote in my theory chapters appear in more recent thesis. It's just that they've probably been written multiple times now, whereas it felt like we were sort of inventing it the first time.

Andrea: That's why I find the Double Diamond quite curious because on the one hand it is a helpful vehicle that enables designers to describe a process. But on the other hand, it's also very limiting. We developed it with a very different conceptual framework than people have used it for. It has been oversimplified in the telling of it and now I think can be a limiting factor in its own right. It is quite interesting how the theories can hold back the practice as well as support it.

Laurene: That's interesting because that comes back to what you were saying earlier around the translation or what happens to a thing when you're endeavouring to expose it, articulate it, position it or make it tangible to someone from a different field.

Andrea: It feels very vague to me. It's one of these things that we have less than satisfactory ways of articulating design's value and process.

Laurene: Having had all this time doing policy work and now being part of the Connected Places Catapult, what do you see as being the continuation of the trajectory of your career?

Andrea: One of the things that struck me about the PhD was it did feel like exercise for the mind. It felt like a fitness regime that you could train your mind to have more flexibility in various ways. The one skill that I think the PhD developed more than any of this is this sense of synthesis and pattern recognition. I feel that is a core skill set that you might see as a transferrable skill set from a PhD and a research base into any field. It is particularly evident in the realm of strategy. For example, the ability to look at complexity, to understand some underlying pattern within the complexity and synthesize some kind of course of action in response to the complexity.

I think I developed this skill very strongly through doing the PhD. I felt physically and mentally different having taken a large document, thrown around these concepts and been able to structure it in a way that was then understandable for others. I think that has continued and I've drawn on that skill set right the way through the Cabinet Office, where again I was dealing with complexities using those synthesis and pattern recognition skills but this time applying them to policy. I was working on a range of government policies but bringing something very different to the other more analytical mindsets much more abductive reasoning of my colleagues, which I think has huge value to other fields.

The Catapult it's a kind of organization that exists to bridge different fields, bringing together research, together with the private sector and government in order to develop innovation. It's almost like a perfect fit for design in many ways. The focus is on innovation so it's about new ideas, and it's about making them happen not just having them. It's that deliverability but it's also about bringing together these different elements into a whole new form on a very daily basis.

Laurene: Do any other members of your team have PhDs?

Andrea: I had anthropologists with PhDs in my former Policy Lab team. But it's curious to me when individuals do Design PhDs, who don't have a design practice background. People who come from economics or from other fields have a very different take on design. There is something very essential, I think, about the nature of being a practitioner and the experience of being a practitioner which is something that I felt as a lecturer I couldn't teach. There were some students, they would go through the same process, but it was not a teachable quality that I could share with them, and other students who had it in abundance and you could literally shape that capacity in them very easily. I can detect it and I think it's a world view as much as anything else. It's always been a curiosity for me around who is a designer, who gets to design that whole labelling of it.

Laurene: You saying this makes me think of the tension that exists for designers as they progress through careers, as to how to find the balance or focus between practice and management or leadership. I remember being told how the engineering firm Arup at one point decided they would have two career paths that people could pursue. You could grow in seniority through your engineering practice as opposed to having to become a manager. Whether or not they still do it I'm not sure, but it was an interesting idea and raises the tension between how we understand advanced expertise for a 'making' practice, and practice or field management and leadership.

Andrea: Jony Ive for example, because he was a few years above me on my undergraduate course, he got to a point in his career where he presumably had to make that decision at Apple. As to whether he ceased to be a practitioner designer and became kind of more in the marketing or CEO side and he chose not to because he is very strongly of the practitioner mindset. He might have a very different view of what a PhD is or whether it is even design. It's interesting because he's now a Rector: Isn't he at the Royal College of Art?

Laurene: When I was selecting people for this project, I wanted to speak to designers who had PhDs. I didn't care what their PhD is in, I just wanted them to have a PhD. It could be by a thesis, it could be by practice, it could be in economics or it could be in typography. Because what I'm interested in is, what does the *experience of doing* the PhD bring them. That's what I think you've been talking with me about is about the skill sets and the things you learn through doing a PhD. Because it doesn't matter if it's by theory or practice, they're all being examined to achieve the same thing. They're all expected to contribute new knowledge in a particular way with a sound methodology that is connected to the literature and existing knowledge in the field.

I think these things are consistent basis for what drives people to undertake a PhD, especially if they don't want to be an academic. We have students at RMIT who are leading practitioners in their fields, who do PhDs in order to deepen knowledge of their practice. Last week I was part of a symposium run in the USA where they were looking at the future of the North American Design PhD (https://www.naphdbydesign.com), and it's so deeply embedded in the conversation that part of the PhD is teacher training. Which means the PhD really is only for people who want to be academics. This approach is a very particular thing to North America, and particularly in the humanities, and it's quite different everywhere else in the world.

By trying to understand why people would want to take on a PhD, I'm really interested in what value might the PhD bring to the maturation of design as a profession, as a discipline, as a suite of disciplines or its contribution to the world. How might a research education support designers in making important decisions, in leading organizations and not just making things look nice. Practitioners with PhDs are common in other domains – we see it in the business world, we see it in sciences and we see it in technology. It's not so unusual to meet somebody in a tech company that would have a PhD.

It is this issue of advocacy that seems to underpin a number of my conversations. I'm quite taken about what you raised in this space of translation and communication, working transdisciplinary and finding ways to do that so that you can achieve your objectives.

Andrea: When I started the research studentship I reached out to British Telecom, to be a co-funder of the Integrated Partnership. I remember writing a proposal to them to ask would they fund this PhD. They were both familiar as a large telecoms company for funding PhDs, and they had done it quite a lot but all through engineering, and they hadn't up until that point sponsored a design PhD. In my proposal I'd said if you fund this then you will have access to PhD level research. They rather sweetly came back to me and said you know what, everyone here has a PhD, you're not bringing anything new. It was very clear to me when I did it alongside telecommunications engineering that that field had embraced doctoral research much more than design. Through the project I was linked into human–computer interaction and design fields.

This was also a time when design research in the purest sense that I'd come from, industrial design, didn't have as strong a community; there was this existing HCI community particularly in the USA. I could read research papers, and it felt like a very legitimate domain of research and scholarship. I always remember finishing the thesis and going to the British Library to have it put on microfiche; I think they do it digital now. That would have been 2005 or so, and they were still doing it on microfiche and I had to select keywords to attribute to the PhD. I scrolled through pages and pages of words around computer science. It was you know, could it be AI or even very subtle, very specific terminology around computers. When I got to the keyword options for design there were only like two or three, and I remember thinking wow this field of computer science has managed to develop this huge vocabulary and research structure in less than thirty years. Yet design has been around in its modern form for more than hundred and hasn't somehow managed to create that legitimacy.

It was really curious to me. Dr Betz had a PhD leading at one time Aston Martin, the car company. It was very common and quite well understood in automotive industry and not necessarily a prerequisite. It was always clear to me as someone coaching undergraduates, a lot of them chose not to do masters because they felt that the legitimate pursuit of their professional impact in the world was to be a practitioner. Their highest order at that time was to go into consultancy, the likes of Apple. To do a masters was not really seen as relevant to design to pursuing it. That was an interesting sort of element, that I would see a lot of talent not going down the research route because they didn't see it as important to their career progression.

In the government I would sit in meetings, with Dr Lucy Kimbell who was at that time our Research Fellow when I set up the team in the Cabinet Office. It was interesting in the early days that if I would say a word like 'prototyping' people would look quite blankly at me. 'What does this mean, what is this thing you're talking about?' But if Lucy as an academic would say yes it's a real thing prototyping and you should look at this paper by X, Y, Z, suddenly the room would be like okay we'll do it then.

I think that really helped in us developing the practice of design in government and policy design specifically where it's added a lot of value. But by coming at it in the way that maybe Tim Brown did with Design Thinking for the private sector. To position design policy in government required, I think the academic rigour. That provided an important platform for the practice to then be actually seen as legitimate and on a par and adding value.

Laurene: That makes a lot of sense to me, which I suppose comes back to the role of the audience and the context that we work in. Finding ways to ensure that people can hear what you're saying or what you must contribute is still one of design's big challenges. Designers typically don't articulate what design does very well which is what Tim Brown managed to do *design thinking*. It made tangible what design that wasn't an artefact or a logo, could be.

I don't think the profession has been able to communicate what they do clearly to clients, especially in new areas of design practice. Yet at the same time I was talking to someone today about my students who were undertaking internships as part of their study. They rarely go and have internships in design firms; instead, they're often in policy, banking, tech, community service or other affiliated industries. These students are going off and doing their placements out in the world, being designers in other contexts rather than going and working in a design studio as their training space. That's been a massive change in the last few years.

I think we're in an interesting time of a schism between design as we've known it as a material practice domain predominantly to design as something else. Designers being able to be and bring something else to important conversations that can inform real change and address real issues that we need to do, it's a different space that we're in now.

Andrea: I completely agree, I do remember at the Design Council, I was working with Chris Vanstone who is based in Adelaide now at TACSI. He and I ran an event, and it was called 'Design is Dead, Long Live Design'. It was trying to get to the sort of essence of what you've just said there around this move away from designs being material into at that time the emergence of service design and design strategy. Some people were calling it invisible design, others were calling it transformation design. It felt again like expanding the context with which design was operating, but also then needing to build that scaffolding and methods. We needed to define what's the practice and what's the research context that sits behind that.

At that time, I commissioned Lauren Tan; she's based in Sydney now at Deloitte but she did her PhD at Northumbria. She'd been at Second Road management consultancy and had been a graphic designer. We were mapping what is service design, and she came at it from a different perspective based on her experience of being in both worlds of design and within the consultancy. I agree that it is really curious how these new practices and contexts have gained momentum in the last few years. I think it probably is in response to shifting need of industry and in a way, I always think design does that. Whether it was its role in the first industrial revolution or the fourth industrial revolution some call it now.

The next big wave in my view, the next ten years will be defined by circular design and what it means for design to play a role in the transformation of the way that we live our lives to meet the Net Zero agenda of sustainable circular design, the circular economy. Whether it is design that changes THE world or whether the economy changes the world and design goes with it. It's quite a curious question to hold depending on your point of view, but I am of the view that those two are intertwined fundamentally.

Where demand goes, design goes, and as design goes along the way it picks up new practices, new methods. The reason I think that is important is that you get all this emergence. These very different fields, you've got service design, you've got interaction design, you've got fashion. But the bigger context within which that sits is the research framework that you would get through doing a PhD, that you get through establishing a coherent research practice that would enable you to understand the value of design per se, as well as the specifics of it in any particular context.

Also, where we talk about domain-independent design, we have to remember that design is very specific when it comes to different fields, you know fashion is very different to car design. But there is a domain-independent part of design that is quite identifiable, which was mostly in the Design Council language the first Diamond of the two in the diagram. The second Diamond, the delivery end is very specific to a field, but the first Diamond was quite common across different disciplines.

I think the big shift I've seen in the last ten years which my research was my first steps into is the transdisciplinary nature of design. Having understood our world, we understand how we might uniquely bring value, then how does that then work with other fields. That's what I think is underneath this sort of trend that you seeing to having designers in at the Treasury in New South Wales or in Canberra, through to designers working in charities, or designers working in the corporate offices of large supermarket chains. It is the value they're bringing to these other professions, these other fields that are transdisciplinary. It's the joining up of all of that and making it make sense for people.

Laurene: I think so, and I think as you say it's been something that's been coming and perhaps now the wave is actually starting to ride a big higher a bit stronger. That there is a greater awareness of the potential of design.

Andrea: I think some time ago John Bessant did some research and he said if you take the argument that design and architecture contribute to about 20 per cent of an economy, that is buildings and products and graphics and so on, but 80 per cent of an economy is services. His argument was if you take the number of designers servicing 20 per cent of the economy and scale that to the 80 per cent (the services) they're not there. He was arguing that we would need millions of service designers in order to meet the service economy. He basically said you need a service designer sat in every seat in every football ground in the UK to achieve this; it was millions of new designers.

What that has meant is that you got a whole bunch of people who aren't designers who are stepping into that field because we literally aren't educating and training enough service designers, we don't have capacity to develop the skills. Which brings us back into the design thinking space about who is a designer and can other people do design and design practice. Which is maybe like people you might be meeting who are designers who have done their PhDs in other fields. That is a really interesting part of your research.

Laurene: It's going to be interesting to see and my aim is to tell the stories, to start the conversations through this work but not to have the solutions. To try and capture this moment as it actually will go forward. Recent research in Melbourne, Australia, has identified that 78 per cent of the total design workforce work in non-design industries.

Andrea: Angela Dumas, who was at London Business School, talked about silent design, and I think she was arguing back in the late 1990s that only 20 per cent of design decisions are made by designers. So, in effect, 80 per cent is made by non-designers, and she wanted to tap into that and influence that. Which again takes us back to this question of should design have a seat at the table; if it does, then what's its contribution? I found myself sat in Downing Street at the table surrounded by scientists and policy makers and you always choose your moment when you're in those kind of environments as to when you raise your hand and what you contribute.

Laurene: Thank you so much for this conversation; there are so many interesting points. This account of your career, and the transition and transformation in your design practice and contribution since undertaking your PhD, has been enlightening. The capacity for design to transform the world and be part of interdisciplinary and transdisciplinary contexts has been enlivening.

Portrait of Chris Marmo

Portrait of Reuben Stanton

6

Practice transformation, collaboration
Becoming leaders

Laurene Vaughan speaks with Chris Marmo and Reuben Stanton

Drs Chris Marmo and Reuben Stanton are co-directors of the design consultancy Paper Giant, based in Melbourne, Australia. They established the business on completion of their PhDs, undertaken at RMIT in two different areas of study – science and design – and different modes of submission and examination, thesis and practice. Both Chris and Reuben came to their doctoral studies after periods of professional practice, including contract research work in the fields of user experience design and interaction design. In the following conversation, they share the influence the PhDs have had on their individual practices and on their joint business and roles therein.

Despite having undertaken PhDs in very different schools at RMIT, their accounts of being embedded doctoral students in funded research projects reveal a commonality of experience and learning. Working with others, including researchers and stakeholders, is a shared experience that has provided a foundation for their roles in their business. Communication strategies, interdisciplinarity and collaboration, which is often about using their expertise to build bridges between disciplines, are shared themes that they reflect on. In this, their experience of doing a PhD has provided a foundation for refining, and continuing to refine, the ways in which they practice, manage and lead.

Community-building, framed through work teams, is a strong theme in this conversation, along with the tools and approaches they have developed to do this. The role of power and seniority in such a dynamic is present but not named. What is interesting is how, as experienced practitioners and doctoral students, they negotiated the complex project teams, integrating the experiences of people and cultures in different forms, and applied new technologies. The skills they developed as students have been pivotal to the leadership and management roles they now perform daily.

A strong focus of a doctoral degree is the research training and outcomes that build the student's capacity to undertake research that is rigorous and innovative. Paper Giant is design research consultancy that works with a breadth of clients and contexts, so Chris's and Reuben's expertise as researchers enables them, in their work with clients, to develop methods and tools that can be used by project teams. But there is something more that they gained from their doctorate experiences that has fundamentally informed and transformed their practice 'for the better', as they say. What is surprising in their reflections is the observation that the PhD sped up their development as designers and leaders. This is surprising because there is a perception that the period the PhD takes – three to four years full time – is long and drawn out, resulting only in theoretical knowing. Their experience suggests that this is not the case. For them, the PhD was an accelerated form of professional development, or practice transformation, that has enabled them to mature as practitioners at a rate faster than they would have through practice alone.

Laurene: Could each of you describe where you did your PhD,
    what your methodology was or how you went about it
    and what the focus of your research was just to give some
    logistical context around our conversation.
Reuben: I did my PhD at RMIT University. It was officially
    in interaction design in the School of Media and

Communication. I was working on a funded research project with a whole bunch of other researchers who were working with a circus company on the design and development of a digital archive. My position in the project was as the only designer working with the project team apart from my supervisors who also had design backgrounds. But in terms of working day-to-day on that project I was doing the bulk of the design work when it came to this digital archive.

Through the practice of doing that, the outcomes of my PhD for me ended up being mostly about design collaboration and different methods to design collaboration with complex teams of people.

Chris: I also did my PhD at RMIT University. I was part of a project called the Affective Atlas Project, which itself was a cross-disciplinary and deeply collaborative kind of project between academics in the design department and academics in the Geospatial Sciences and Mathematics Department within RMIT University. My position on that project was that I was based in the geospatial science department within the university and was on a day-to-day basis collaborating with people that called themselves geographers and cartographers and other sorts of more hard science place-based practitioners and GPS experts and these types of folk.

I was probably one of the only people in that group to have an actual cross-disciplinary PhD myself where my purpose was actually to combine different disciplines through the thesis itself. The project was in partnership with Parks Victoria, who are a state government body here in the state of Victoria in Australia. They are responsible for managing National and State Parks, what we can call public green space. I did an ethnographic study with them looking at how their understandings of place and space were playing out when it came to land management and technology use. I brought a design lens to that and helped frame up some different ways of thinking about what technology does and how it's used when it comes to managing land.

So the actual piece of paper that I got out of the PhD says 'land management' on it which to me doesn't really describe what I do at all. I don't even have a garden. I live in an apartment. What I've taken out of the PhD is a very deep introduction to and training in social science research methodologies. I started off with a human–computer interaction lens over the project, and through the course of the research turned it into something closer to human and cultural geography and design rather than human–computer interaction.

Laurene: It's interesting for me to hear you both describe the teams that you did your PhDs with, which to my mind presents something that's very different to what a lot of people talk about the doctoral experience as. Typically, the PhD is described as being an extremely lonely and isolated experience, where the student is on their own and occasionally meets their supervisor. However, what I was hearing is that there was this other communal, collaborative and interdisciplinary team and contributors around your study.

Having heard what you did, I'm interested to know – what do you think you learnt? Not so much about land management or circus archives, what else do you think you learnt by going through and completing the PhD?

Reuben : It's a big question. I can have a go at a couple of things. What I tell people who are not academics if they ask that kind of question, I say that I learnt how to do research properly and what research is. I don't know if I can tightly define that for you. But what I feel like I've been able to bring to research work outside of academia is an understanding of what it means to set up a line of inquiry and turn the inquiry into something. And to be able to direct that research process with purpose and including defining some boundaries around the inquiry.

Not getting distracted or ever feeling like – and this is something you hear from design research practitioners a lot including my staff or people that I work with, is this feeling like of 'I don't know if I've even done enough research'? I never have that feeling, because I know from doing the doctoral research that it's impossible to ever do enough and to find out everything about everything. All you can ever do is take a step forward in your inquiry and your knowledge. So that's a thing – it's not like I haven't learnt *something* – I learnt research techniques and I learnt how to analyse data and work with qualitative and quantitative measures and things like that.

But ultimately, it's about being able to understand that there are ways of finding out stuff about the world that will help you, and I don't think I really knew that before I did the doctoral research. I hadn't done research in that kind of way before. Does that make sense what I'm saying?

Laurene: To me it does but I'd be interested from Chris if that's . . .

Chris: I agree with everything Reuben has said regarding what he got from his PhD. I certainly got that too, but I think I would like to call out some further differences maybe in our careers up to that point. I'd worked as a user experience designer and researcher, primarily a researcher, in the lead-up to my PhD. When I started, I found myself in this strange position of having done a fair amount of commercial research, especially the super practical day-to-day skills of conducting an interview and sense making and synthesizing findings. I felt like I had those skills developed in the commercial area or I had to develop those myself. I had some grounding in what it meant to do research and how to go about that and I think that's actually how Reuben and I met.

We were both hired as Research Assistant positions at RMIT before our PhDs, myself as a user experience researcher and Reuben as a user experience designer. Coming at the PhD with those slightly different backgrounds was interesting because I felt like – I'd had the title of researcher in my previous job roles but on reflection I just recognized the different sets of blinkers that I had on when it came to my research practice. A key thing that I took from a PhD was a deeper sense of collegiality not just with current peers and practitioners but with a history of a discipline that I hadn't had much formal training in before – which is the social science discipline.

I understood the origins, history and evolution of the tools that I was already using in my professional practice as a qualitative researcher. I felt more grounded in that and felt connected to a deeper vein of knowledge and practice because of that. I felt like I was able to create the time and space to make those connections for myself through the PhD. Out of that depth came that realization that Reuben's articulated just now, which is understanding what it meant to do research that was grounded in what had happened before. Research that was very explicit and deliberate about the methodologies and tools that were being applied to it, and the constraints that were inherent in the problem and not just constraints provided by the context like time and money which is often the case in a commercial context.

That was a different thing for me, and I think I actually learned what it meant to be an interdisciplinary practitioner through doing the PhD. I'd had a mixed background in my undergraduate studies. I'd studied different things for different reasons, and I think the PhD helped me thread together a lot of those different lines of inquiry into something that felt like it had a more solid theoretical and philosophical foundation for the first time. The PhD really helped me understand a lot of what had already happened in my career up to that point. It enabled me to make sense of it and has continued to provide me with a feeling of stability, confidence and ease with the work that we do. I just didn't have before the PhD.

Laurene: That's very interesting. In some ways what I'm hearing is you're saying that the PhD experience enabled you to contextualize a practice and to consolidate your knowledge and experience. It seems like that is present for both of you. In a way that it's because you had research experience or a practice orientation beforehand that you brought *into* the PhD and consequently you weren't complete novices in doing research. You had some embodied practice knowledge and relationship to that in place, and the intense period of study allowed you to put into some . . . order might be the word to use . . .

Chris: Yes.

Laurene: Some kind of order that you are then able to draw on. With this in mind I'm interested in moving into the next part of the conversation which is, how has this informed where you are now? How has that experience supported you or enabled you to be where you are now, or not?

Chris: Well, I think I can speak for both of us. Reuben and I are both running a design consultancy called Paper Giant – we're founders of the company and have different types of managerial positions within that company. But I think to answer that question of, what do I think would be more difficult about my job now, if I didn't have the PhD? I think I wouldn't be able to confidently mentor a lot of our staff through the complexities that they encounter in the work. We do quite a lot of research-led design work. In fact, almost all the projects we do are in that category. We even have quite a few projects which I would call closer to something like social research rather than design.

Often, we're not really designing anything out of the project. We're focused on helping an organization of some kind – government or private sector, understand something about the world and use that understanding to some end.

I don't think I could be as confident a practitioner either
advocating for approaches or navigating stakeholder
opinions without that deep connection that a PhD gave me,
to the practice and the history of what we do. That's one
part of it – advocating for what I believe and know to be the
right approach to a problem or the right way of navigating
through it. Also just having the knowledge of what to bring
into a conversation that will help that conversation progress.

I think knowing how to talk about research approaches
and their validity is vital from a client point of view and
in developing the team dynamics. I find myself mentoring
some of our more junior staff members through qualitative
or design research approaches, and I feel I wouldn't be able
to do that in quite the same way without that PhD training.
I should note here that I didn't really explicitly teach during
my research. I know a lot of people have that experience,
but I didn't have much teaching experience built into my
PhD time. Nevertheless, I still feel much better prepared to
mentor people through complexity because I feel like I've got
a better foundation to stand on myself.

Laurene: That's based on what you've been through yourself?

Chris: Yes. I think the story of my PhD was in stitching together
different disciplines and figuring out where my affinities lay.
I did this by trialling, trying on and discarding or reiterating
different kind of world views. My personal learning journey

in the PhD was one that started off in a very positivistic kind of science-based mindset which is what my undergraduate degrees were in. I studied computer science and psychology, so very different disciplinary foundations to where I ended up in the journey of the PhD. For me it was a journey of discovering the empirical nature of the social sciences which I just didn't learn in my undergraduate studies because I didn't study those things explicitly.

Discovering that whole new body of knowledge and world view and methodological toolkit helped me contextualize the practice in the way that you just summarized. It also gave me the confidence that I know how to make the argument for a particular approach as a legitimate way of building knowledge and a legitimate way of navigating a particular type of problem. Before this, I would have had an intuition that a particular tool or approach was useful, and I would have had over time enough experience to develop deeper knowledge through a design practice or a research practice. But without that PhD experience of deliberate exploration and reflection, and mentorship and support from those teams I was studying with, I wouldn't have made the same connections or come to the same understandings.

I feel like I got to these realizations much quicker than I would have otherwise. I think that's an interesting and

important counterpoint to make to the common criticisms
of a PhD that it might be time consuming or too long. I
genuinely feel like I got to a much better understanding
faster by studying this explicitly and deliberately than
I would have gotten on my own. Without that focus
and dedicated learning space it would have taken me
decades to understand what I learnt. I just wouldn't have
known how to create the space or time to learn what I
did otherwise.

Laurene: Interesting. Reuben do you want to share
    your experience?

Reuben: I agree with everything that Chris said. It's interesting
    to think about specific kinds of methodological stuff
    because my PhD was explicitly a PhD through practice. I
    was working as a practising designer with a team of people,
    who were again a cross-disciplinary kind of group. My PhD
    research within the living archive project was about explicitly
    reflecting on that practice and trying to figure out what I was
    doing and what was going on in the team and through my
    contributions. This included the theoretical underpinnings
    behind those actions. As Chris said, it was through this
    process that I came to this really solid understanding of
    really specific kinds of tools and techniques for working
    with teams. This included the ways and modes of being as
    a designer in a group of people who were trying to make

decisions about things. This is what I wrote a big chunk of my thesis about.

Doing that reflection in the research enabled me once again to shortcut my understanding of 'what's all this stuff that a designer can do in these kind of spaces?' I was able to really, directly just lift that discovery and apply it to other design situations that I now find myself in. This includes working with complex groups of people who come from diverse disciplinary backgrounds and trying to decide together about something that they're trying to make. The PhD basically gave me this big toolkit of things that I had a level of understanding about and that I was then able to apply to different situations, without having necessarily worked in the same context before in the way that other designers might have had to, in order to be able to understand what to do in that situation.

To be a bit more explicit one aspect of my PhD was about how designers – myself – used particular kinds of visual artefacts in order to be able to get people to a shared understanding of something so that they could make a coherent and ethical decision about what they're going to do next in the project. Through having done that research work and understanding how design tools can work in different contexts, I'm able to bring that mode of thinking to other contexts and say, 'Okay these people are all trying to do this thing, what kind of visual artefact should I make that's going to help them do that thing?' Or, 'what can I experiment with in a way that's going to help them or how could I learn better to understand that the thing that I'm using is working?'

Rather than say I'll use this design toolkit or this textbook that I've read that says that maybe I should use this thing in this situation, but not necessarily have a clear understanding of why I should use it. I have a richer and evidence-based approach. The PhD has given me the confidence to be able to be quite experimental when it comes to using visual and other communication artefacts within a design practice working with big organizations. The reason I have that confidence is that I know how to identify whether or not, the thing I'm doing is working or not, in a structured and even empirical kind of way. I know what kind of things to pay attention to and what sort of data I'm collecting to know whether or not what I'm doing is working and if it's not working, I'll try something else rather than kind of barrelling ahead thinking, 'This is the technique we use at this particular part of the design process so that's what we're going to use' even if it's not leading to the outcomes that the client has asked for.

Laurene: What I find interesting is, it seems that both of you are talking about how your PhDs have given you a confidence to be able to do things. Confidence about your approach to practising and your approach to knowledge discovery. I suppose it's a kind of humility or an acceptance of not knowing everything and an adaptability. Is that a fair way for me to position it?

Chris: Yes. For me that's true. It definitely gives you humility, but also the counterpoint to that is the confidence in knowing that you understand that you don't understand – or that you don't need to understand everything. I think there are two elements for me. The PhD taught us a way of establishing a process of inquiry and a confidence in that process and the confidence that we could change the process. This includes being able to navigate complexity with others. There is a confidence that I think we both developed through that. For me there's also a very pragmatic and practical set of tools that the PhD gave me as well.

Whereas Reuben is saying that he took a range of methodologies with him from his study, for me the thing that I took from my research was a completely different language or metaphors, and as a result a completely different way of understanding the world that I just couldn't have come up with myself. The endpoint of my thesis was in generating design principles that are more spatial and grounded in place and space, and in the way that we understand our connection to each other and environments that we're working within and moving through.

Those metaphors have been instrumental for me in terms of thinking about how you design a company like Paper Giant for instance. I found my PhD research to be an endless resource for me to think through not just how to deliver client outcomes or good design outcomes but how to think about designing the rhythms, spaces and processes that Paper Giant is made up of, in order to support others to do that work too. It's given me individual confidence in following a process but also a set of very, very useful thinking tools that have proven themselves to be quiet versatile I think in the same way that Reuben has been explaining.

Being able to apply those frameworks or those theories or those understandings to different contexts is the main benefit of my PhD experience. It's always really fascinating to see the applicability of what we've learnt or what I've learnt into completely different areas.

Laurene: I'm very interested to hear more from you regarding how your PhD sped up an area of your expertise and how that has impacted on your careers particularly how you perform your roles at Paper Giant in terms of being Directors – and managing people. I'd like to explore this a little more and how is it for the two of you working together, because you have a lot of synergies but you have quite different backgrounds and approaches to things as well.

Reuben: I don't know if there are links between, for me anyway, from doing the work in the PhD and the kind of work of running and managing a company. How closely they're connected other than in the sense that we take a very design mindset to the company itself and are willing and able to redesign. As Chris was saying before, we design the way the company works as we go. I think some of that comes out of the kind of mindset we each took from the PhD. We tend to look at everything as a research project and treat it as an opportunity to learn more about something and then respond to what it is that we're learning as we go.

Laurene: I suppose I should have been clearer about that intersection. It's not just doing the doctoral work or being a PhD student working in teams. I'm wondering if there is any link or correlation that you could make to the design management, design leadership kind of literature proposition that's in the world and the areas that you also practice in.

Reuben: I feel like I learnt a lot from doing the doctoral work around communicating to different audiences in different ways and producing things that would help people understand complex problems. Understanding complexity and being able to respond to that is something I bring that to my management practice. But I don't know if there's a direct correlation or not between having done doctoral work or worked in any other kind of context for three years straight. Doing the doctorate was the first time I'd worked in a single job for more than eighteen months in my career. I don't know how much of it is just concentrating on something and learning how to work with a group of people really closely, and the things that I learnt from doing that which I could have learnt somewhere else, and how much was the PhD itself.

There's something interesting you said about Chris and I being quite different, having different disciplinary backgrounds kinds of training and different ways of approaching things. We reflect on this quite a bit. We are quite complementary, and we have quite different kind of management roles within the business.

My role is very much about managing in much more of a short-term time horizon in relation to the day-to-day: working with individual people and managing different business functions and designing them. Tracking the health of the business and communicating that back out to the staff and working with staff in that kind of close way.

Chris's role focuses on the longer-term time horizon, looking at more of the longer-term business strategy and tactics at a much higher level. As well as the role that he kind of described as being a mentorship role when it comes to research and our research practice specifically. I think that those two things work together and play off each other. That's kind of where I see things being, do you want to add anything there Chris?

Chris: I think that's a good articulation of the differences. I do think the type of management we do would be more difficult if neither of us had a PhD. I think we wouldn't be able to embrace a collaborative and iterative mindset as easily, especially when it comes to business practices. People find that surprising when they join us, just how open and inclusive the decision-making is, and how collaborative the design project, that is, the company, is. People are generally surprised by that and enjoy it. Well, some people do. Some people like other management styles where it's like where someone tells you this is what we're doing and why and just do what we say.

It's been interesting over the last couple of years to learn how our management style has been influenced by design. I think we are definitely designers first and managers second as Reuben has alluded to. We are learning how to be managers on the job. The other thing that I think we need to note is that I understand Paper Giant to be a site of enquiry and research itself. In my role it's mostly my job or my kind of inclination to think about where we might head in say six to eighteen months' time rather than the next couple of months. This is important for us to navigate the competitive landscapes of business or to understand the types of problems we might be being asked to solve and think about by clients. Especially what we would need to do to prepare to solve those problems. Whether it's bringing in different skill sets or learning different tools.

I think my job is about translating that understanding of the world, including all the usual business things like competitors and opportunities and all that stuff. Keeping an eye on that and translating that into Paper Giant as a site of inquiry, and then working with Reuben and the rest of our team to understand how we want to iterate and improve Paper Giant in response to what we see in the world. We do this with an explicit understanding that Paper Giant itself is an intervention in the world towards a particular purpose. I think we often revisit that purpose and adjust it based on where we think the world is at and where it might be heading and what types of problems might be available to us to solve and what types of problems need us to help with them. I think that's something that comes quite naturally to me now because I have that toolkit available to me in terms of understanding themes, trends and opportunities out in the world.

I can draw upon my research training to help me understand the competitive landscape and the way that the market might be changing. During the Covid crisis, for instance, I found we were pulling together threads across disparate sources and trying to use these insights or make a value judgement very quickly around whether something is useful or just noise. This is something that you do in a PhD, and I think that skill set has been super valuable, not just through Covid but through the history of the company so far and that's what I enjoy applying to Paper Giant. Helping the business navigate changing contexts, translating that context into the company and then also working with Reuben to make the company itself a better intervention in the world.

Laurene: It's interesting as you both speak I hear your two foci of your research underpinning your different perspectives. I'm finding myself going to de Certeau, and contemplating strategies and tactics and how they play out as a complementary action between the two of you. Because your respective knowledge dispositions and how they inform how you work.

I'd like to pick up as a final thing. You raised it just then and it's about values and the ways in which values inform what we do. It's not necessarily something that we explicitly name in doctoral training but is always present – that is values around knowledge production. What matters, what doesn't and this is informed by what the individual researcher's catalyst for what they want to do or what they want to study is. I've framed this as, *what do you want to know and what do you want to do*? I think is fundamental to identifying the focus of a PhD for someone. Because from the answers to these two questions you can work out what you want to know and how you want to go about knowing that. It's very basic terminology but it is effective. I think there is a values layer to this that guides how the research comes into being. So, I'm wondering about values and if they are important to what you do.

Chris: It is there definitely. Values for me are tools to think with. We've certainly articulated values to ourselves and they have certainly evolved over time. They haven't changed too drastically. I think they are relatively fixed, but they exist on spectrums as well and we do move up and down those spectrums in response to the world. They're in dialogue with the strategy in that kind of classic de Certeau take on the relationship between strategy and tactics.

For me we articulate what those values are, and we communicate them to our staff. But I think for me they are design interventions themselves. They're tools to think with, they're tools to make decisions with. They're tools to communicate a culture and a direction to our team. I think that's where I have come to learn of their value most of all in terms of helping someone decide whether Paper Giant is the right place for them to join as a practitioner. But then in doing a lot of the communication work that is vital in a team even of our size around what we are doing and why we're doing it.

For me I've already talked about how for us Paper Giant has been a very deliberate attempt to make an intervention into the world towards a particular purpose. Again, we can talk to what that purpose is but I think the values are complementary to that and help us communicate to ourselves and our team around why we're doing what we're doing. Of course, they also help us find the right people to partner with in the world from a client kind of point of view too. They do a really good job of sorting out whether client relationships are going to be the right ones for us. They're kind of the things that sit between different spaces for me, using the spatial metaphors again, they're kind of themselves kind of thresholds that people communicate through and around.

Reuben: The thing that's maybe important to add, as you mentioned when we started Paper Giant, pretty much as we were wrapping up and graduating from our PhDs. We didn't just start Paper Giant because we like designing and wanted to do this kind of stuff. There are lots of other things we could have done, but I think over time it's kind of become clearer as to why Paper Giant exists in the world. We're here because we think the world could be better and we think society could be better. We've got a definition of what better actually means:

that definition is 'a more just, and more equal, and more sustainable society'. We try and do things that enable that. I think to connect this back to the doctoral work, we came into this with a hypothesis that applying interdisciplinary skills and interdisciplinary craft through design would be a way to help organizations deliver better policy and products and services – according to that definition of better.

In practice that looks like research and design consultancy work, but it's all underpinned by those values and this particular approach that we're trying to get the world to change because design tries to change the world in small ways and in big ways. We're intervening in the world by making things, or by helping other people make things, and that's all with this frame around it of we're trying to help people make the world in a certain way. We think that applying this kind of combination of skills and knowledge is a way to achieve that.

I didn't know that I was interested in that before I did my PhD. Or I had a feeling that something about the work that I was doing prior to my PhD which as you mentioned was primarily software and UX work wasn't achieving the right kind of things for me or in the world, but I didn't know how to articulate what kind it was. I think the PhD did help give me a language to think through it and I've now landed on a language where I can describe it.

Chris: I think maybe to stitch our kind of two parts here together, this is how we understand it. Reuben is providing a lot of the content around the function of the principles and for me I'm really fascinated in recognizing that they're tools to think with. Right now, I think we have a really strong alignment in helping organizations 'deliver better'. But we're doing a lot of thinking about how the tools themselves are vital to get people within the business aligned with why we're doing what we're doing. Helping others understand that purpose without having done or gone through the same experiences that Reuben and I have is challenging. They're doing a lot of heavy lifting in terms of communicating or distilling an understanding of the world that we both developed through the PhD for us to staff but also to clients.

They're important tools when it comes to maintaining organizational health. People need to understand, they need to hear from Reuben and I quite regularly what that is. What those values are, what our purpose is and as I've already mentioned we also use it as a way of deciding which clients to take on or not, as well. They help us find the right partners for us when it comes to making the change that we want to make, so that we're not barking up the wrong tree.

Reuben: There's just one other little thing that I want to say, I don't know where this fits into the conversation, but you asked a little while ago about Chris and I working together and how us both having PhDs fits into that. I think there is something that's quite important about the fact that we both have done doctoral degrees. Through that I'm able to understand what Chris is talking about when he talks about his 'research orientation' towards the company. I don't think it would be the same if only one of us had that kind of training.

Even though our research degrees were quite different from each other, there were as I said some crossovers. Just knowing what it means to have done a PhD and what that does to your brain. I think we can understand each other and why we might be talking in a certain way about something or taking a certain approach with something, or trying to apply some theory to some other kind of context. We are able to create space to allow that kind of experimentation to happen as well. I don't think that would have been possible if it had only been one of us who had that kind of training.

Laurene: Have you recruited any people with PhDs into your team?

Chris: Yes we've had a couple. We've had two or three others with PhDs in Paper Giant. I think just being able to trust that they've got the type of research training that we have is a great thing. So just to use some examples. I can think off the top of my head, there might be more who had PhDs who aren't in the team now. One of them had a social science background and the other one more of a public policy background. I found working with them really similar to working with Reuben. There is a whole bunch of vocabulary and thinking and frameworks that you can, not take for granted, but more easily assume in common. You're able to get to a more productive place quicker.

If I just talk about it myself as an employer now – we do get applications for positions within the company quite regularly, often unsolicited ones not applying for roles or jobs, and we're in a very fortunate position to attract people in that way. We feel really humbled that people do that, but we do see a lot of resumes and cover letters and portfolios. For me, people with a PhD stand out almost always because I know what they're coming to a position with a research base, that is different to someone who doesn't have that.

I'd say that even those that have done masters degree. I just find myself with a bit more affinity towards people that have done a postgraduate research degree because I understand what they can bring to Paper Giant because we ourselves are those people. So that would be my point of encouragement I guess for anyone thinking about it for their job prospects. We understand how you can translate some very deep skills across domains and disciplines quite easily.

When I've seen other organizations in a similar field approach those same people, they read what's on the tin and what's on the tin might be 'land management'. They don't understand what else happened behind that and I feel like I've got a much more empathetic and understanding of people's experiences having gone through it myself. I understand that it's more or less – there is a lot of overlap even in the kind of disciplinary cousins when you're doing a PhD. I feel like we're more easily able to draw out those threads and think about how we can apply them through our purpose.

Laurene: That's really the nub that I'm trying to understand and to be able to communicate through the various interviews. I want to understand and be able to communicate what is that transferable knowledge and expertise that a PhD gives you.

Chris: I have seen some, not anxiety, but kind of reticence or maybe lack of confidence in some PhD applicants to jobs around that transferability. But I think because both of us came from industry before we studied, I think that transition back out for us was a bit easier than it is for some other people.

Laurene: Is there anything else you would like to add, say, share as we come to the end?

Chris: I would just end my part by saying undertaking a PhD does change the way you think about the world fundamentally and for the better in my case. I do think about things completely differently now and I'm really glad and the PhD was instrumental in that.

Reuben: I'd say something very similar, like the way that I work as a designer was fundamentally changed by doing the PhD, and I think it was changed for the better.

7

Discovering self-leadership through research

Following is a list of the PhDs of the six designers interviewed for this book:

1   Emma Jefferies, 'Fostering Designers' Visual Practices through a Sociocultural Approach'.

2   Daria Loi, 'A Suitcase as a PhD? Exploring the Potential of Travelling Containers to Articulate the Multiple Facets of a Research Thesis'.

3   Chris Marmo, 'Reframing Space for Ubiquitous Computing: A Study of a National Park'.

4   Dimeji Onafuwa, 'Design-Enabled Recommoning: Understanding the Impact of Platforms on Contributing to New Commons'.

5   Andrea Siodmok, 'An Investigation into
     Communication Studies to Improve the Designer's
     Understanding of the Virtues and Constraints of the
     Three-Dimensional Graphical User Interface'.
6   Reuben Stanton, 'Acts of Design: Archives, Material,
     & Intention in the Circus Oz Living Archive Project'.

Interviewing the six designers for this book has given me the opportunity to learn more about the nuances of doctoral education and design PhDs through first-person accounts. The topics with which the designers engaged reveal the many synergies and differences between the research projects they undertook. Most are in design in its broadest sense, and many address issues of technology, people and interdisciplinary contexts for design application.

I have deliberately not shared their PhD thesis titles until this point in the book, as they provide only one view into the PhD. They draw attention to the research and the subsequent scholarly contribution that each designer has made; they do not tell us anything about the experience of *undertaking* a research degree, nor what each candidate has taken away from the years of research and subsequent outcomes. Often titles are abstract, developed through a frame of keywords that will support library searches. They may also refer to the funding agent behind the PhD studies.

My intention in this book is to expand this view of the PhD, to discover what these six individuals experienced and what impact it has had on their professional lives. As I undertook the interviews and then reflected on the transcripts, I could see common themes emerging from their diverse experiences. It is, of course, possible that what I observed is not what others will in their readings of the conversations.

This is not in any way a conclusive list of what a PhD student can expect to experience, nor does it signal the areas of expertise and the strengths that they can expect to have on completion. The experience is different for each of us. Although the content or focus of the research has not been expanded upon in this text, I have observed, and experienced through my own post-PhD trajectory, that the topics we research and the passion we develop for a very specific area of study or method of research do not stop once you complete. Decades after completing my own PhD, I continue to draw on aspects of what I learnt through my research at that time, bringing it to bear on my own continuing practice and research.

Curiosity, process and practice

Arguably, these three aspects – curiosity, process and practice – are fundamental outcomes of a research-training degree, and they should be. They are among the attributes and skills we expect to be evident in a PhD submission, a suite of tools that anyone undertaking research needs to have.

Curiosity drives an enquiry. It represents the desire to know or to discover, and it is evident in the research process through the questions or propositions that guide the enquiry. It is an ongoing catalyst for new knowledge, projects, opportunities and growth.

Process is linked to methodology and to the twists and turns of discovery that occur during a research project. It is something to which you must hand yourself over, suspending worries about the outcome in order to embed yourself in what is unfolding. Research and researchers, as some of these conversations attest, don't always end up where expected. It is the disposition and commitment to enquiry and discovery that pushes practices and projects forward and transforms them.

Practice refers to expertise that is in a constant state of evolution. Designers who undertake PhDs through practice find themselves interrogating the very practice that is also the means for the research. In this context it is akin to the verb to practice. Across all disciplines and professions, it is increasingly related to expanding ongoing learning and development in a particular area of expertise. No matter the driving relationship between the research and design, the experience of undertaking a PhD impacts on the practice of the designer-student, through the application of new knowledge, evolving research skills that spark applied curiosity, and through consideration of how we do what we do and how it connects to the work of others.

Christopher Frayling's publication *Research in Art and Design* (1993) presented a case for research in art and design being undertaken either through, for or about some aspect of the practice. In 2019, I debated this separation and proposed that it is possible during research study that the researcher embrace all three postures in one project. The conversations in this book make evident that the impact of research training will continue to inform an approach that can expand beyond projects to more general intentions and ambitions within the practice.

Resilience, communication, advocacy and agency

The designers all spoke to the topics of resilience, communication, advocacy and agency, qualities that are often referred to as soft skills. These were something the interviewees learnt or refined through doing their PhDs, something they had to develop as a result of their studies or as something they had an ambition to engage with post-graduation.

The so-called softness of these skills is grounded in the personal, emotional and values basis that underpins and enables them. It could be argued that core research skills – undertaking a literature review, refining a research topic and questions, designing a study and producing outputs – are all hard skills of research. They have established metrics and expectations. The soft skills are the desirable dexterities of *being* a researcher, designer or just simply a human being, living in the world. As such, they are harder to teach, as they are more often enabled. They may emerge from a supportive learning environment – or in a reaction to one that is not. They are what the designers interviewed here have taken from their degrees and applied to their practices.

There are many accounts of how difficult it is to complete a PhD. In fact, it is not uncommon for PhD students to not complete, and programmes the world over seek to establish ways to prevent this. The PhD is a long degree, and the relationship with one's supervisor or adviser is equally long. Much happens in a person's life over the span of the study and beyond it.

Loneliness is often cited as one of the key emotions many students experience and that derails them in their ambition to finish. In the conversations with designers here, several share accounts of how important the community of students was to their success and to the richness of their overall experience. Friendships are forged through a close understanding of what fellow students have done and gone through. Dimeji advises that an important part of a potential PhD student's decision to enrol should be identifying who their study cohort will be. Daria shares that the challenge for her of not conforming or fitting in with expectations. Eventually, she found a supervisor who was her advocate and fellow students who were her allies. She drew on the support of her community, and trust in the integrity of the process, to have the resilience required to stay true to her research focus. In this we can see that resilience is grounded in people, relationships and conviction.

Throughout their studies, doctoral students learn a range of communication skills, beyond the material practices of communication. Typically, these focus on communication of the research process and outcomes through publication and other forms of dissemination, such as presentations and lectures. The interviewed designers talk to another communication skill honed through their studies: the capacity to communicate across disciplines and through layers of hierarchy to achieve their research aims. I would hypothesize that this is grounded in necessity (the need to get project work done) and commitment (personal drive to achieve research aims). Reuben shared how for him this transitioned from a necessity in the large, funded research project within which he did his PhD to the focus of his research in the project – specifically, the design tools and methods he could use to keep a project moving and to build shared understanding across disciplinary boundaries and power structures.

Emma reflected on how her personal experience of living with dyslexia was the mainstay of her research and her ongoing design consultancy. For her, it was about developing or refining a different literacy skill set through visual literacies and communication. Through this and the opportunity to join design studios globally in the research for the book *Design Transitions: Inspiring Stories. Global Viewpoints. How Design Is Changing*, Emma honed her focus on empathy and an awareness of difference. She thereby built her own resilience, expertise and capacity to work across contexts. Andrea expands on this through her reflections on working in a range of government agencies where she sought to find a shared language and understanding of issues and processes that works across disciplines. For her, building connections between design, policy and economics is a key area of focus and contribution. Learning how to strategically communicate, using the tools, methods and contexts that enable it, is part of this.

Leadership

The soft skills and personal and strategic transformations outlined above represent areas of capability that make up many professional development programmes and publications. These are the skills that leaders and colleagues are expected to have to realize and bring about change, or, as Dimeji noted, design for good/impact. In the various conversations, each designer talked to leadership, sometimes explicitly but often implicitly, through their commitments, ambitions and broader contributions to their fields. It is not unreasonable to think that developing specific advanced research and topic expertise will advance your opportunity to be a leader. In some areas, it is a requirement for a particular professional, but this is new to design.

Leadership and new models of leadership are dominant themes across nearly all sectors of work and practice. Through their doctorates, projects, roles in teams and post-PhD employment, each interviewee presented their approach to and models of leadership. It is easy to think that leadership is aligned to role, but the concept and its opportunities far outweigh such boundaries. Designers can be leaders in their domains through their material practices, through community-building and advocacy groups and through the ambition to transform the way we design. To me, this is one of the strongest contributions to ongoing practice that the doctoral experience has provided.

Chris and Reuben state that their PhDs accelerated their leadership capacity and ability to establish and run their own design consultancy. Emma presents a case for a more focused way to lead, and for her it is through commitment to empathy and expanding our understanding of design practice – who it is undertaken with and for whom. Similarly, Dimeji commenced his study with an ambition to further contribute to design and to his design contexts. Through the PhD, he has gone on to significantly contribute to the decolonizing design movement, in conjunction with transition design for social, economic and environmental transformation.

Daria presents a robust case for self-leadership and, from this, leadership through design and across fields. Since completing the PhD, she has forged new areas of interdisciplinary design practice and scholarship, and she sees her role as a leader as one of enabling others. Andrea shares a similar commitment to design's potential to transform worlds in the manner that Daria does. Both during and after her PhD she has, through a range of roles, led others in their pursuit of design and design value.

In *What Is a Designer* Norman Potter stated that 'No book about design is politically value free . . .' (Potter 1989: 7) and that 'design is a field of concern, response, and enquiry as often as decision and consequence' (9). The reflections and insights shared in this book show that this is the case. The commitment of the designers to practising design in a manner that adds value, makes the world better and is inclusive is a prime example that Potter's early definition, in terms of design scholarship, continues to be accurate even as the practices, contexts and technologies of design have expanded significantly. There are those who would argue that designers merely realize the ambitions of clients, which is and isn't true. There are too many variables in the world of design to make such universal claims. But what do Potter's claims mean for a designer thinking of taking on a research degree such as a PhD? What impact will the time spent reading, reflecting, conversing and learning with and from others have on practice per se?

A characteristic of PhDs undertaken through practice in art, design and architecture is the ongoing process of critique in the advanced research programme, and it should be noted is not unique to them either. Peer review is another form of critique that takes place across all academic fields and is the basis for doctoral training and ongoing academic work.

After many years of participating in doctoral critiques, my observation is that this honest, interested engagement between student and critics is both challenging and a great reward. In the world of practice there is an element of critique, but often positioned against the client brief. In a PhD, the focus isn't on the outcome and its applicability to a brief but on process and discoveries themselves. These sessions can be both invigorating and profound, for this space of peer review is almost nostalgic for the early days of undergraduate studies. But unlike in that scenario, the student being critiqued brings an established body of knowledge and practice to the project under review. David Maeda says of the process: 'critique teaches you to listen hard to others' criticism so you can listen harder to yourself' (Maeda 2011: 28). Not all the designers in this book experienced the critique process during their doctoral studies, but it is easy to view the PhD as resembling a grand critique – one that takes years and has many inputs. It has profound impacts on the person listening, learning, writing and endeavouring to make a contribution to knowledge in their field. What struck me most as I reflected on the conversations is that leadership is a dominant thread across the designers' experiences, and it has informed who they have become as designers. This is, I think, the most profound impact that a PhD will have on a designer. It encompasses their ability to be a researcher, their expert knowledge of their topic and their leadership in that field through their research contribution. These are the known areas of leadership and expertise that a PhD will bring. Beyond this is the personal transformation that comes from developing and adopting a richer way of being a designer.

In 2022, Rama Gheerawo published a collection of case studies of design leadership. In the opening chapter, Gheerawo points out that 'Leadership is often seen as a professional accomplishment, with little attention paid to personal development' (2022: 19). I wonder what this means for designers undertaking PhDs. Based on the conversations in this book, it is clear that leadership is nuanced and not always about a position; in the case of these designers, the PhD was a profound form of personal and professional development.

The proposition that doctoral education is a form of leadership development deeply connected to the practices and contexts of design is what drove me to write this book. It is something I have observed among my own PhD students, even when they came to their doctoral studies as experienced designers. I did not set out to prove this idea through these conversations; in fact, it is not something that was raised as a point for discussion. It emerged as I analysed and reflected upon the conversations. Perhaps it is best framed as personal leadership, which is itself the embodiment of the hard and soft skills of working with others, of being resilient and curious.

At a point in time the discoveries from the PhD are at the forefront of knowledge and research on a specific topic, but this is quickly be built upon and surpassed by the work of others. It is a reality that all researchers must accept and the nature of academic work. It does not diminish the importance of the work. It endorses it, for as others build on one's work, it becomes part of the material of their progress. Such is the process of research.

I named this chapter 'Discovering self-leadership through research', as I observed this to be the common thread that emerged through the conversations with these six designers. The term 'self-leadership' originally emerged in the organizational studies literature. In 1983, Charles Manz coined the term to articulate a person's motivation to do and achieve things within a work context with minimal direction from others. In this way it is akin to what we may refer to as drive, mission or focus within a career. The reflections of each of the designers in this book evidence their commitment to their individual passions and concerns as designers. I use the term self-leadership to refer to embodied leadership that is based on values and the conviction to have positive impact through technical and interpersonal expertise. Each of these designers has their own commitment to contribute to the world, one that is grounded in their experiences of undertaking their PhDs. It is what drove them to undertake them in the first place, as well as their ongoing career developments post-study. The rigour and challenges of their doctoral studies, and their passion to contribute *through* their research and expertise, appear to have been a robust mode of professional development that has enabled them to be design leaders of others, of their fields and of themselves.

I often counsel potential students to think about what they want to know and what they want to do. Fundamentally, I am asking them to articulate why they want to pursue this challenging and at times confronting, mode of study. What value or addition will it make to their professional lives beyond pursuing excellence in what they already do? Sometimes they respond with a desire to know more about a topic, or they believe that the qualification will enable them to get better jobs, be promoted or will enable them to become an academic. I have never heard a student articulate that they want to grow as leaders in their fields as people rather than technical expertise. Self-leadership for many is the surprise outcome. The rigour, duration and passion (sometimes obsession) that the PhD demands has an impact on our personal and professional selves. I cannot lie and say that undertaking a PhD is easy, because it isn't. But from my personal experience and that which I have observed in others, it is impactful in a manner that is beyond the research project.

Recently I was having a casual conversation with a colleague, who is an engineer with a PhD and not an academic, about this book and its progress. They declared, 'I would not have had the career I have if I didn't have a PhD. Sometimes my roles have required it, but it's more than that. It is the resilience you develop to defend and make your case for your ideas that has served me.'

SUGGESTED READING LIST

Some further reading suggestions

The following is a list, in alphabetical order, of books that may be of interest if you are thinking of undertaking a PhD. They connect to the themes in the book. This list is in no way exhaustive. Not all disciplines are covered, nor specific topics. All the publications are available online, hopefully through your local library. I hope that they will help you find what you are looking for. Once you start searching, all manner of things emerge. If you search through an online publication database, you will also find many articles and videos of presentations on the topics covered in this book. Increasingly things are OpenAccess.

Design leadership

These publications bring together a range of approaches to design leadership, building on the insights from the designers in this book.

1   *Creative Leadership: Born from Design*, Rama Gheerawo. United Kingdom: Humphries Publishers, Limited, 2022.

2   *Redesigning Leadership*, John Maeda. Ukraine: MIT Press, 2011.

3   *Design Leadership: How Top Design Leaders Build and Grow Successful Organizations*, Richard Banfield. China: O'Reilly Media, 2015.

4   *Design Leadership: Securing the Strategic Value of Design*, Raymond Turner. United Kingdom: Taylor & Francis, 2016.

Doctoral education

The following is a list of publications that provide insights into different models of doctoral programmes across disciplines and countries. They include some reflections from students on the experience.

1   *The Creative PhD: Challenges, Opportunities, Reflection*, Tara Brabazon, Tiffany Lyndall-Knight and Natalie Hills. United Kingdom: Emerald Publishing Limited, 2020.

2   *The New PhD: How to Build a Better Graduate Education*, Leonard Cassuto and Robert Weisbuch. United States: Johns Hopkins University Press, 2021.

3   *The PhD at the End of the World: Provocations for the Doctorate and a Future Contested*, Denise Cuthebert

and Robyn Barnacle. Germany: Springer International Publishing, 2021.

4 *Getting the Most Out of Your Doctorate: The Importance of Supervision, Networking and Becoming a Global Academic*, Mollie Dollinger. United Kingdom: Emerald Publishing Limited, 2019.

5 *The Idea of the PhD: The Doctorate in the Twenty-first-century Imagination*, Frances Kelly. United Kingdom: Taylor & Francis, 2017.

6 *The Practitioner-researcher: Developing Theory from Practice*, Peter Jarvis. San Francisco: Wiley, 1999.

7 *Changing Practices of Doctoral Education*, Alison Lee and David Boud. United Kingdom: Routledge, 2009.

8 *Reshaping Doctoral Education: International Approaches and Pedagogies*, Alison Lee and Susan Danby. United Kingdom: Taylor & Francis, 2012.

9 *The Realities of Completing a PhD: How to Plan for Success*, Nicholas Rowe. United Kingdom: Taylor & Francis, 2021.

10 *Doctoral Education for the Knowledge Society: Convergence or Divergence in National Approaches?* Jung Cheol Shin, Barbara M. Kehm and Glen A. Jones. Germany: Springer International Publishing, 2018.

Creative practice and research

The following selection of publications presents insights into the ways in which creative practice and design are being used within formal research contexts.

1   *The Creative Reflective Practitioner: Research Through Making and Practice*, Linda Candy. United Kingdom: Taylor & Francis, 2019.

2   *Creative Research: The Theory and Practice of Research for the Creative Industries*, Hilary Collins. United States: Fairchild Books, 2018.

3   *Interacting: Art, Research and the Creative Practitioner*, Ernest Edmonds and Linda Candy. United Kingdom: Libri Publishing, 2011.

4   *Artists with PhDs: On the New Doctoral Degree in Studio Art*, James Elkins. United States: New Academia Publishing, 2014.

5   *Doctoral Research in Art*, David Forest. Australia: Australian Scholarly Publishing Pty Limited, 2017.

6   *Design Research Through Practice: From the Lab, Field, and Showroom*, Ilpo Koskinen, John Zimmerman et al. Netherlands: Elsevier Science, 2011.

7   *Visual Research (Second Edition): An Introduction to Research Methodologies in Graphic Design*, Ian Noble and Russell Bestly. Switzerland: AVA Publishing, 2011.

8   *Associations: Creative Practice and Research*, James Oliver. Australia: Melbourne University Publishing, 2018.

9   *Creative Practice Research in the Age of Neoliberal Hopelessness*, Agnieszka Piotrowska. United Kingdom: Edinburgh University Press, 2020.

10 *Doctoral Experience: Student Stories from the Creative Arts and Humanities*, Donna Lee Brien, Craig Batty and Elizabeth Ellison. Germany: Springer International Publishing, 2020.

11 *By Practice, by Invitation: Design Practice Research in Architecture and Design at RMIT*, Leon Van Schaik and Anna Johnson, 1986-2011 (The Pink Book). Spain: Actar, 2019.

12 *Practice-Based Design Research*, Laurene Vaughan. India: Bloomsbury Publishing, 2017.

13 *The Routledge International Handbook of Practice-Based Research*, Craig Vear. United Kingdom: Taylor & Francis, 2021.

14 *The Routledge Companion to Design Research*, Joyce Yee and Paul A Rodgers. United Kingdom: Taylor & Francis, 2014.

15   *Provoking the Field: International Perspectives on Visual Arts PhDs in Education*, Anita Sinner, Rita L. Irwin and Jeff Adam. United Kingdom: Intellect Books Limited, 2019.

16   *Practice-led Research, Research-led Practice in the Creative Arts*, Hazel Smith and Roger Dean. Germany: Edinburgh University Press, 2009.

Design knowing/expertise

This collection provides some insights into the nature of design knowledge and knowing through action. It includes some publications that have investigated the nature of design and its practices, in practice and as research.

1   *Analysing Design-Activity*, Nigel Cross, Henri Christiaans and Kees Dorst. United Kingdom: Wiley, 1996.

2   *Designerly Ways of Knowing*, Nigel Cross. London: Springer-Verlag, 2006.

3   *Design for Transformative Learning: A Practical Approach to Memory-Making and Perspective-Shifting*, Lisa Grocott. United Kingdom: Taylor & Francis, 2022.

4   *Design and the Creation of Value*, John Heskett, Clive Dilnot and Suzan Boztepe. United Kingdom: Bloomsbury Publishing, 2017.

5   *What Designers Know*, Bryan Lawson. United Kingdom: Taylor & Francis, 2012.

6   *How Designers Think: The Design Process Demystified*, Bryan Lawson. United Kingdom: Elsevier Science, 2014.

7   *Design Expertise*, Bryan Lawson and Kees Dorst. United Kingdom: Taylor & Francis, 2013.

8   *Learning in Practice: Insights from Community, Workplace, and Higher Education*, Jack Mezirow and Edward W Taylor. Germany: Wiley, 2011.

9   *The Reflective Practitioner: How Professionals Think In Action*, Donald A Schön. United Kingdom: Basic Books, 1983.

10 *Design Research: Synergies from Interdisciplinary Perspectives*, Jesper Simonsen, Jørgen Ole Bærenholdt and Monika Büscher. United Kingdom: Taylor & Francis, 2010.

11 *The Ontology of Design Research*, Herrera Batista and Miguel Ángel. United Kingdom: Taylor & Francis, 2020.

12 *Design as Research: Positions, Arguments, Perspectives*, Andreas Unteidig, Florian Conradi, Gesche Joost, Katharina Bredies and Michelle Christensen. Germany: Birkhäuser, 2016.

13 *Ideograms*, Leon Van Schaik. Australia: Lyon Foundation Limited, 2013.

REFERENCE LIST

Brown, T. (2009), *Change by Design; How Design Thinking Transforms Organisations and Inspires Innovation*, Boston: Harvard Business Press.

Cardoso, S., et al. (2022), 'The Transformation of Doctoral Education: A Systematic Literature Review', *Higher Education*, 84: 885–908.

Cross, N. (2007), *Designerly Ways of Knowing*, Boston: Walter de Gruyter GmbH.

Frayling, Christopher (1993), *Research in Art and Design*, London: Royal College of Art.

Gheerawo, Rama (2022), *Creative Leadership: Born from Design*, London: Lund Humphries.

Grocott, L. (2022), *Design for Transformative Learning: A Practical Approach to Memory-making and Perspective-shifting*, Oxon: Routledge, Taylor & Francis Group.

Hill, D. (2012), *Dark Matter and Trojan Horses: A Strategic Design Vocabulary*, London: Strelka Press.

Jefferies, E. (2021), 'The Story of Emma Jefferies', *Blue Sky Republic*, February. Available online: https://www.listennotes.com/podcasts/the-space-in-between/the-story-of-emma-jefferies-YK6dqIshWV0/.

Maeda, David (2011), *Redesigning Leadership*, Cambridge, MA: The MIT Press.

Manz, C. C. (1983), 'Improving Performance Through Self-Leadership'. *National Productivity Review*, 2 (3): 288–97.

Potter, Norman (1989), *What Is a Designer: Things, Places, Messages*, London: Hyphen Press.

North American PhD by Design Symposium (2013), Carnegie Mellon University, USA. 5 October. Available online: https://www.naphdbydesign.com (accessed 20 February 2023).

Rittel, H. W. J. and M. M. Webber (1973), 'Dilemmas in a General Theory of Planning', *Policy Sciences*, 4 (2): 155–69. Available online: https://link.springer.com/article/10.1007/BF01405730.

Schon, D. A. (1983), *The Reflective Practitioner: How Professionals Think In Action*, New York: Basic Books.

Stappers, P. J., et al. (2022), 'Guiding the PhD in Design. Experiences from Six Programs', in D. Lockton, et al. (eds), *DRS2022: Bilbao, Conference Proceedings, 27 June–3 July*, Bilbao, Spain. Available online: https://doi.org/10.21606/drs.2022.845 (accessed 16 March 2023).

Thackara, J. (2007), *Dott07*, London: Design Council. Available online: https://www.designcouncil.org.uk/sites/default/files/asset/document/dott07.pdf.

Vaughan, L. (2017), *Practice-Based Design Research*, London and New York: Bloomsbury Academic.

Vaughan, L. and A. Morrison (2014), 'Unpacking Models, Approaches and Materialisations of the Design PhD', *Studies in Material Thinking*, 11: 1–19. Available online: http://www.materialthinking.org/papers/159 (accessed 1 March 2023).

Wildman, G. (2021), 'On Tradecraft: The Practice of Strategic Design and the Role of Trickster', PhD Thesis, RMIT University, Melbourne.

Yee, Joyce, Emma Jefferies, and Lauren Tan (2013), *Design Transitions: Inspiring Stories. Global Viewpoints. How Design is Changing*, Netherlands: Laurence King Publishing.

INDEX